The Goodnight Book

RICHARD BEWES

CHRISTIAN **FOCUS**

Copyright © Richard Bewes 2009

Paperback ISBN 978-1-84550-465-6
epub ISBN 978-1-84550-670-4
mobi ISBN 978-1-78191-037-5

10 9 8 7 6 5 4

First published in 2009,
Reprinted 2010, 2012 and 2018
by
Christian Focus Publications,
Geanies House, Fearn, Ross-shire,
IV20 1TW, Scotland.
www.christianfocus.com

Cover design by Moose77.com

Printed and bound by
Bell & Bain, Glasgow

MIX
Paper from
responsible sources
FSC® C007785

INTRODUCTION

'I'M LIKE A LITTLE CHILD,' I said to my friend, Ken Taylor. 'I just don't like bedtime at the moment!'

Millions would concur with my experience at some point in their lives. The action-packed day that makes 'winding down' difficult, the fear of what 'tomorrow' may bring; pressures on the marriage, in the workplace or family; decisions looming ahead, the heaviness of grief - or the sheer trauma of moving house!

On this occasion for me it was a health challenge. It can be very reassuring to have a world-travelled professor of heart surgery visiting you as the dreaded evening begins to close in. Ken Taylor was wearing a dark suit that I could only describe as 'formidable.' Evidently he was on his way to an important appointment. He nodded and smiled at my remark. He was all sympathy.

– 'You're never forgotten,' he declared. 'And before we part, I'll share something with you to boost your spirits and help you along.'

But I'll save what Ken Taylor imparted to me until chapter 14.

Meanwhile, *The Goodnight Book* is intended for ... well, pretty well anybody – of whatever philosophical or cultural background. It's said by psychologists that the last thing we think about at night tends to stay with us, and become a part of the subconscious, thus affecting our mental and emotional make-up. So here it is, one page at a time - one word of truth per evening! Or less frequently if preferred.

Pressure at work, then? ... moving house? ... health concerns? ... bereavement of one's spouse? ... traumatic decisions? They've all happened to me. And usually it is at night that I tend to have been at my most fragile.

I am grateful to Linda Nikitin and her sister Kath in Michigan, USA, for their helpful checks and warm encouragements in the writing of this book.

I wish you peaceful reading.

RICHARD BEWES
West London, England

1

'And there was evening and there was morning, one day'
(Gen. 1:5)

Literally translated, the sentence reads, *And it was evening and it was morning, day one.* Here was Creation – and the order in the book of Genesis is interesting; evening first, then the morning! Following this progression from the twilight to the light, the Jews traditionally calculated their day from sunset to sunset.

We can do the same – and particularly at those times when we may find ourselves reluctant to face the approaching night. Learn to view the onset of the evening, not as the dregs of a dying day – but as the prelude to another day of adventure on Planet Earth!

Professor Leonard Bacon of Yale University said about the night times of life, 'Blessed are they who at such times have learned to "look forward and not back."'

There is no need to view the night as *negative* switch-off time, certainly not as far as the Creator is concerned. 'The darkness and the light are both alike to Thee,' wrote David (Ps. 139:12 KJV). Jesus once declared, 'My Father is *always* working, and I too am working' (John 5:17).

By day and night, heaven is never off duty

2

Moses, one of the greatest leaders in all history, wanted to see the glory of God - but learnt that no one could see God's face and live; the sight would be too overwhelming. 'But', says the Lord, *'there is a place by me.'*

Moses takes a look – and there is a mighty rock. He'd known about rocks before. There had been *water* from the rock at one point in his adventures. Moses had once *sat* on a rock as he prayed for victory from his enemies. Now he was to *stand* on a rock – and be hidden in its cleft as the glory of God passed by.

These rocks all amounted to one and the same thing. Centuries later the New Testament pointed to *'the spiritual rock'* that accompanied God's people in their adventures – 'and that rock was Christ' (1 Cor. 10:4).

Whenever people of faith look for support, for a place of permanence and protection, you can be sure that the rock we are looking for will turn out ultimately to be a Person.

That is where we can come at the deepest moments in life – to that very place, right beside God – hidden and secure in Christ Himself.

Rock of ages, cleft for me,
let me hide myself in Thee

3

'Who is weak, and I am not weak?'
(2 Cor. 11:29 KJV)

My dad was a church minister, and one day - wearing his clerical collar - he boarded a train. A passenger smiled at him.

-'Wouldn't you agree,' he suggested, 'that really religion and faith are only for the weak people of life; those who need God as some sort of crutch to lean upon?'

Dad smiled back. 'You're right!' But then he went on, 'And *I'm* weak. In my life I've faced pressures that I could never have come through without the power of God. And how about *you?* Are you strong?'

Suddenly the man's composure collapsed. He was at that moment on his way to the divorce courts, his personal life in shreds. You can be sure Dad gave him all the help he could.

It's when we think we're strong that we are most likely to topple. *Power through weakness* is a theme taken up in the Scriptures by the Christian apostle Paul. And in many songs!

I am weak but Thou art strong;
Jesus keep me from all wrong;
I'll be satisfied as long –
As I walk; let me walk, close to Thee

4

'In quietness and confidence shall be your strength'
(Isa. 30:15 KJV)

We saw it in Ken Rosewall, a diminutive Australian, who at one time ruled the world of professional tennis. Head down, he would trudge back to the baseline for the next point – and the magic would settle on him once more for another classical rally. Nothing rattled him. Sometimes close friends, maybe a coach, would call to him from the sidelines; he rarely heard them. Rosewall's mind was completely occupied elsewhere.

Such capacity for inner stillness was coveted - on a corporate level - by the prophet Isaiah for his own people of Judah twenty-seven centuries ago. They were supposed to be God's own people ... but they were distracted from their true loyalties by their frenzy for an unreliable Egyptian alliance. *Return to your roots,* was his plea. 'In returning and rest you shall be saved.'

And quiet – on the individual level? Evening time is useful for the setting aside of a day's events – some days are busy and happily crowded; others are uneventful, frustrating and hard. It's back-to-the-Creator time – and the learnt development of an inner quiet with Him at the end of a day... *regardless of what is happening around us.* In that way lies re-creation – and peace.

'God is the friend of silence'
(Mother Theresa of Calcutta)

5

*'Take therefore no thought for the morrow:
for the morrow shall take thought for the things of itself.
Sufficient unto the day is the evil thereof'*
(Matt. 6:34 KJV)

These words are stamped indelibly upon the human race in hundreds of languages. Three times in His sermon Jesus used the phrase – *Take no thought* – as He referred to the anxieties people feel about food, livelihood, clothing and life itself.

It's not that men and women should act irresponsibly. It's rather that – *having taken such precautions as we can* for our selves and our close ones – we should then stop worrying, and let tomorrow bring what it will! Once we entrust the *centre* of life to the Creator, we can learn to trust Him – about everything.

After a talk that I once gave on BBC, a businessman wrote to me. He had been dreading the next day, and happened to switch on his car radio just as I was ending! All he got were my last seven words – a quotation from the celebrated Gospel singer, George Beverly Shea, at the time of his eightieth birthday. They were, *'Fear not tomorrow; God is already there.'*

A difficult interview ahead? Hospital surgery? A college exam? If we can get centred upon God and His love for us, we can echo a phrase from the Swahili language of East Africa, made famous in a song from the film *The Lion King:*

'Hakuna Matata' – *No worries!*

6

The night following the Lord stood by him, and said unto him,
"Be of good cheer, Paul"
(Acts 23:11 KJV)

The night following.... What night was it? Why, here was Paul the apostle, a top-security prisoner of the Romans, having been dragged that day out of a violent demonstration, and facing an assassination plot the very next day. Yet in the middle of the turmoil, there was the presence of Jesus beside him.

We don't read of the Lord *arriving* in the jail. He was just *there*. Around were the solid walls, the bolts, the chains – and armed guards. But nothing can keep Christ out of any place at all!

Where are you right now? Whatever the happenings of your past day, it's over. You're now into 'the night following.' Put up a prayer of trust, that – whatever happened in the last twelve hours, and whatever you could be facing tomorrow morning – the unseen presence of Christ will draw close to you at this moment, in friendship and encouragement.

It happens anywhere. It is international. Toyohiko Kagawa of Tokyo, who worked in the slums of Kobe, once wrote, 'The deeper my little life is buried the more I feel that Jesus is my Friend. The carpenter Jesus is my Guide. He is my Saviour.'

'The darkness deepens; Lord with me abide'

7

'Are not all angels ministering spirits?'
(Heb. 1:14)

I was in a bad way, gasping for breath, my car drawn up in the forecourt of a petrol station. I had no strength to call for help. let alone move from the car. It was a quarter to midnight.

-'Can I help you?'

It was a woman at my car door. Where had she come from at that hour – with all the risk of approaching a stranger? Soon she was beside me, in the adjoining front seat – a calming, supportive presence. Her name was Pauline. Other help was forthcoming. Friends of mine, Jim and Petra, phoned from home for an ambulance. Them I knew well. But not Pauline.

The ambulance came – and Pauline was out of the car, waving it down. From its interior I managed to wheeze, 'Thank you, Pauline, Thank you!' She disappeared into the darkness.

'I think she was an angel,' said Petra later. I wouldn't disagree. Biblically an angel is simply a *sent one*. God has His ministering spirits at hand – in hospitals, at battle fronts, even in petrol station forecourts. You may not be a spirit-being as such – but is it possible that God may send *you* one dark night, to someone needing His help? I hope Pauline will see this page.

'The angels are nearer than you think'

(Billy Graham)

8

*'Stand at the crossroads and look; ask for the ancient paths,
ask where the good way is, and walk in it'*
(Jer. 6:16)

What to do, when faced with pressing dilemmas? They come to nations and individuals. Jeremiah's advice to his wayward listeners twenty-six centuries ago should be applied today.

The prophet suggests four action points. STAND, when you are at the crossroads of decision – do *nothing!* Ten minutes' thought may be enough. That gives time to LOOK – at past mistakes, and lessons learnt – for the next time! And then?

ASK for the well-trodden previous paths that brought earlier generations happiness and stability – in business, in marriage, at church and through the Scriptures. *Ask* of wise people who have been around a while. *Ask,* supremely in prayer, of the Lord God Himself: *YOU know which is the good way; show me!*

The conceited can never do this; they think they know best – and so they *run,* headlong, into unwise strategies, alliances ... and mounting problems. The humble among us will WALK – that means with steady, tested decisions – into the future.

Did Jeremiah's listeners take his advice? Not a bit! He was just about the most faithful preacher in history – and the most unheeded. His listeners continued on a disaster course.

Ten minutes' thought is enough to change a life

9

'The disciples left ... rejoicing because they had been counted worthy of suffering disgrace for the Name'
(Acts 5:41)

Disgrace? Why, they had been severely flogged. It wasn't the miracles of healing by the early Christians that so upset the city authorities. It was the *preaching* that was doing the damage! Before long there were going to be martyrs.

Bishop Stephen Neill once wrote, 'Throughout the centuries, the Church of Christ has survived only because there has been within it a sufficient number of men and women who were willing, if need arose, cheerfully to die for Him.'

Is there someone reading this page at the end of a day's harassment – because you are a believer? It must indeed be hard ... *but you are in honoured company*. Bearing scars – physical or mental – for Christ's Name are *honourable scars!* You are part of a movement that will never be rubbed out.

'There is a pleasure,' wrote Blaise Pascal, 'in being in a ship beaten about by a storm when we are sure that it will not founder. The persecutions which harass the Church are of this nature.'

Can he have travelled far, who hath no wound, no scar?
(Amy Carmichael, 1867–1951; missionary in India for 55 years)

10

'The Lord is my Shepherd'
(Ps. 23:1)

Prayer sometimes flies out of the window. It can happen in hospital;, during some personal trauma, or in the face of bereavement – when the spirit goes numb, and words refuse to form. The psalmist put it expressively: *I am so troubled that I cannot speak* (Ps. 77:4 KJV).

The believer need not feel guilty when prayer goes silent. There are times when we simply don't know what to say. For the time being we can remain in a comfortable silence with the Lord, and allow others, who know us and love us, to do the praying.

But even in the direst extremity, there is still a prayer that *can* be used. *The Lord is my Shepherd.* Five words only – for the five fingers of your hand. Count off the fingers, beginning with the thumb, and match them with the five words of David's prayer. When you reach the word MY, you have reached the fourth finger. Pianists call it the 'weak finger' – and that stands for *you,* in your present fragility. *Hold onto that fourth finger with your other hand.* You can keep grasping it in bed as night descends, accepting that it is the Lord, the Shepherd of your soul, who is Himself keeping a tight hold upon you.

I've tried it. You try it….

'In the darkest hours He is still with us'
(G. Campbell Morgan)

11

'You will not fear the terror of night'
(Ps. 91:5)

Fears become accentuated at night, and can oppress even the strongest and bravest. I have known periods when I have slept with a Bible under my pillow – not as a charm, but as a tangible reminder of the God who, in this psalm, pledges the watchfulness of His angels upon those who *'call upon Me.'*

The Lord's help is described as 'the shelter of the Most High','the shadow of the Almighty', 'refuge and fortress', 'shield and rampart'; even the 'wings' of a hen over her chicks.

Sometimes just one person can bring God's help. An example was Florence Nightingale, the fearless pioneer of modern nursing during the Crimean War. In the hospital wards she was known as 'The Lady with the Lamp.' Many foundations were named after her. *But there is a more permanent Lamp.*

In a TV debate the celebrated journalist Malcolm Muggeridge declared, 'My impulse, when the darkness sweeps me up, is not to say, "Please let me out of the darkness", but to seek the light which I know is there.... I look for the window, *and Christ is the window.'*

All terror recedes. God's all-seeing vigilance over His people was once described as –

'The saints' candle which never goes out.'
(C.H. Spurgeon)

12

'Your Father knows what you need before you ask him'
(Matt. 6:8)

We children looked on confidently as our Dad fixed the worn carburettor on the ancient Ford V8. We were travelling on holiday from Nairobi to Dar Es Salaam – but the nearest garage was a hundred miles away. No matter – any true missionary was trained to strip down a car engine! Later that journey, it was a matter of crossing the Wami River – *with the bridge in bad repair*. We got out and watched as Dad roared across the flimsy planks in top gear. 'He's risking his life!' we chirped with shining eyes. It was the same when the rains churned up the roads – 'Dad is *good*, driving in mud!' In his care for us all, Dad was always far, far ahead.

Human parenthood at its best is, in the teaching of the Scriptures, patterned after the Person we have come to recognize as 'the God and Father of our Lord Jesus Christ.' Although the term *Father* had been used earlier by Jewish people – almost as a national title – it is to Jesus' teaching that we owe the intimacy associated with this, the Name by which we best know God. *Our Father* .... It is unique to Christianity.

'Whatever the crisis'? Yes, *whatever*. A book was once written, *I Dared to Call Him Father*. Under God's fatherly care for you, know tonight that *He is far ahead*. Begin 'Our Father ...'

'He combines fatherly love with heavenly power'
(John Stott)

13

'Give your servant success today by granting him favour in the
presence of this man'
(Neh. 1:11)

'This man' was none other than Artaxerxes, Persian Head of
State; the most powerful man around. And Nehemiah was
just the butler – but he was also a believer, yearning to help in
the rebuilding of Jerusalem's shattered walls, 500 miles away.

How to get permission to go, with an unpredictable man
– and potential oppressor - as your boss?

Try prayer! Many people try prayer *last*. Not Nehemiah.
The book of Nehemiah is peppered with his one-sentence
'arrow prayers' – anyone can pray those. And notice what
prayer did to Nehemiah's view of his superior! The mighty
Artaxerxes is reduced to the level of 'this man'.

Prayer cuts the most powerful person – or problem – down
to size. Is there someone formidable that you are dreading to
meet tomorrow – head of department, family member, even
your consultant? Prayer teaches us to see them as God sees
them – *minus* their trappings of power – just as vulnerable
people with ulcers, in-growing toenails or failed relationships.

'This man ... this woman.' *Prayer does that.* Nehemiah got
his wish eventually, and went to bed happy. His book tells
the rest.

'It is prayer, and prayer alone, that can make history'
(Jacques Ellul)

14

'The Lord is the strength of my life'
(Ps. 27:1 KJV)

This is the Scripture given me by Ken Taylor, on my admission once to hospital. The verse stayed with me throughout.

'We want you out of bed, Mr Bewes; we want to weigh you!'

Weigh me, oh no! Then the verse would come to mind and I would totter to the wheelchair scales and sit on them.

'No, no, Mr Bewes; you *must* raise your feet onto the foot-rest; start all over again!'

Oh goodness; it's impossible. Lord, I need your strength!

What tiny issues; heaving back into bed, reaching for a tissue, getting out of the bathroom! But huge, when your world has shrunk to a single room and you haven't strength enough even to hold a cup of tea. Your eyes are irritated by the glaring fluorescent lighting overhead, your ears endlessly tormented by bleeping monitors and the chatter of visitors across the ward, your wrist sore from umpteen inserts into your 'line'....

I clung to Ken's verse more than any other. Now it's precious, and it's my turn to share it with *you* – wherever you are.

'God worketh in you, therefore you can work'
(John Wesley)

15

'I, Paul, the prisoner of Christ Jesus'
(Eph. 3:1)

Are you reading this in some kind of prison? The apostle Paul was in a *real* jail. But he wrote not as a prisoner of Rome, but of *Christ* – and used his cell to write part of the Bible!

Similarly, John Bunyan, 350 years ago, wrote *Pilgrim's Progress* from the jail where his preaching had brought him.

Some people feel themselves imprisoned within the four walls of their home, or immobilised in sheltered accommodation. Others, like the beloved quadriplegic Joni Eareckson Tada, have described their *bodies* as a kind of prison.

It's Christ who creates the turn-around. He is a real and living person who, when invited, will come into our lives and share them with us. Kate Booth, daughter of General Booth of the Salvation Army, once found herself in a Swiss jail because of her witness, and there wrote her famous Prison Song:

'Best beloved of my soul, I am here alone with Thee,

And my prison is a heaven, since Thou sharest it with me.'

We too can make an *arrangement* with the Lord for our daily surroundings – even our bodies – to be a sanctuary fit for Him.

'My wheelchair ... my passport to adventure!'
(Joni Eareckson Tada)

16

*'All we like sheep have gone astray; we have turned every one to his
own way; and the Lord hath laid on him the iniquity of us all'*
(Isa. 53:6 KJV)

My most important night ever, I was listening to a Mr Nash.

'Suppose,' he said, 'that the light above me represents God;
that my right hand represents Jesus, and my left hand represents
us. And now' – he placed his Bible on his left hand – 'suppose
this dark object – forgetting that it's a Bible – stands for all our
sins and their deserved penalty, weighing us down; Now!' – he
looked at his left hand and began to quote Isaiah 53:6. I was
only thirteen but I got the point – *we've all sinned.*

Then the speaker looked up at the light. 'And the Lord,' he
continued - and he transferred the black object from his left
hand to his right – 'hath laid on *him* the iniquity of us all.'

'Where are your sins *now?*' he asked. I got it - why, *Christ*
at the Cross had borne them instead of me. I told the Lord
that evening how sorry I was for my sins that He had borne;
that I wouldn't keep Him out of my life a minute longer! The
Bible calls this Repentance. Earlier we had sung these words:

There's a way back to God from the darkness of sin;
There's a door that is open, and you may go in;
At Calvary's Cross is where you begin,
When you come as a sinner to Jesus

17

'Remember me when you come into your kingdom'
(Luke 23:42)

What a difficult moment in which to believe in Christ! The thief, dying on the cross next to Jesus, had no religious background, knew no prayers, and was unable even to turn his head and see his fellow sufferer. But amid the agony, the heat, the thirst, the flies and the jeering of the onlookers, the goodness of Jesus had registered with him. He'd heard Christ's prayer for the Roman soldiers: 'Father, forgive them, for they do not know what they are doing.'

Unlike his fellow-criminal on the other side of Jesus, the penitent thief – as he has come to be called – felt his heart melting. One step of faith – and he was there, with his gasping attempt at a prayer, *Remember me; take me with you!*

It was enough. It is always enough. In paradise who might you *expect* to see at the very side of Jesus? Moses? Elijah – or brave John the Baptist? It was to a man out of the very gutter that Jesus said, 'Today you will be with me in paradise.'

'With *Me*....' Such is the power of Christ. There on the Cross – in His greatest extremity – He still had the power to draw the most unlikely person to Himself, and into an eternal security.

'Love so amazing, so divine, demands my soul, my life, my all'
(Isaac Watts of Southampton, 1674–1748)

18

'Near the cross of Jesus stood his mother'
(John 19:25)

Mary, the mother of Jesus, would have known that this was what her Son had come for. She and Joseph were to call him *Jesus* ('Saviour') at birth, 'for he shall save his people from their sins.' Earlier, Mary had received a prophecy that 'a sword shall pierce your own soul also.' *The moment had come.*

The sky went dark, the earth rumbled; even the graves of Jerusalem were disturbed. As the Jewish Christian Alfred Edersheim wrote, 'A shudder ran through nature.' Jesus – God in human form – was suspended between earth and heaven as He hung upon the Cross. The earth was rejecting Him with its cry "Let him be crucified!" *But heaven was rejecting him too* as God's just wrath was vented upon human rebellion – declaring in effect, 'There's the cheat! There's the slanderer, the murderer, the paedophile, the swindler!'

God in Jesus Christ was intercepting His own judgment upon sin. It was an act of purest love – that we might escape judgment. At that point Jesus was the loneliest person in the universe.

'Near the cross of Jesus stood ...'. Why not put your own name there? Identify with Christ in His dying love for you. God says, *I'll meet you at the Cross; nowhere else. I will forgive you only on the basis of my Son's death for you, as you trust Him.*

The Cross becomes Judgment Day, already past!

19

'Abide with us: for it is toward evening, and the day is far spent.
And He went in to tarry with them'
(Luke 24:29 KJV)

The statue of Lew Wallace, an American author, soldier – and one-time Governor of Utah – is situated in the U.S. Capitol, in Washington DC. Years ago Wallace began some research, hoping to explode what he felt to be the 'myth' of Christ's resurrection. But his wife was a believer, and she prayed ....

The research progressed, but led the writer irresistibly to the conviction that *the story of the Gospels was true*. The day came when Wallace got on his knees and submitted his life to the risen Christ. Wallace's wife persuaded him to continue the book – which was to become a classic entitled *A Tale of the Christ*. Later still it became the all-time famous film, *Ben-Hur.*

Here is Luke – another researcher! – who writes of the two travellers on the road to Emmaus, on that first Easter Sunday evening; of the Stranger who joins them and accepts their invitation to 'abide' with them for supper. Then, in His familiar act of breaking the bread, they suddenly realize that the Christ of Calvary's cross is in fact their ever-present Lord of Easter.

'Abide with ME,' runs the hymn. *It's personal.* Around the world today there are at least two billion people, convinced of the companionship of Jesus with them, by day and every night.

The resurrection gave Calvary wings to fly!
(Bishop Festo Kivengere of Uganda)

20

'For God so loved the world that he gave his only begotten Son,
that whosoever believeth in him should not perish,
but have everlasting life'
(John 3:16 KJV)

'I thank God for this word *Whosoever*,' said the seventeenth-century preacher, Richard Baxter. 'If it read "There is mercy for Richard Baxter," *I* am so vile that I would have thought it meant some *other* Richard Baxter; but this word "Whosoever" includes the worst of all the Baxters that ever lived!'

Taking up this point, I once was explaining John 3:16 from a pocket Gospel to a very sick man in hospital. 'Put your own name in there, Ken,' I encouraged. "God so loved *Ken*, that he gave his only Son, that as *Ken* believes in him, *Ken* should not die, but *Ken* should have everlasting life." Can you put your trust in Christ, in this way?' I showed him the passage.

Ken could hardly speak, but by way of answer, he picked up a ballpoint, found the verse – and put a *tick* in the margin. His meaning was unmistakable. He had committed himself to Christ, and his arms went round my neck in gratitude to God.

True 'believing' is more than intellectual assent. John 1:12 shows us that believing is the same as 'receiving' Christ – into the centre of life, as Saviour, Lord and God!

'I once was lost, but now am found'
(from slave trader to hymn writer; John Newton, 1725–1807)

21

'He hath said, "I will never leave thee nor forsake thee."'
(Heb. 13:5 KJV)

Bible scholars tell us that in the original Greek language of the New Testament, a *double* negative – like 'No, never!' – is the strongest possible way of *affirming* something. Then I heard someone say that in Hebrews 13:5 (where the Lord promises his followers that he will never abandon them), we are faced not with a double negative, but with a *quadruple* negative!

Well, I had to look it up for myself. Sure enough; there it was. Literally translated, the sentence is: *'No, never* (double negative) *will I leave you; No, never* (double negative) *will I forsake you.'*

It's a relief to know it, and especially when someone, however tentatively, has put their trust in Jesus Christ as Saviour and Lord – only then to experience hardship, opposition … and perhaps *doubt*. We find ourselves saying, 'I don't *feel* that Christ is close to me. And I have let Him down so much that by now He must have given up on me.'

No … never! In John 6:37 Jesus said, 'Whoever comes to me I will never, no never *(double negative)* drive away.' Take it on trust. Regardless of our failings *or* our feelings, Christ does not change His mind once we have come to Him. Believe it tonight.

It's therapy for the soul – a quadruple negative!

22

'Hear my cry, O God…. From the ends of the earth I call to you;
I call as my heart grows faint'
(Ps. 61:1, 2)

Beloved Ruth Graham, Billy Graham's wife, once told of how their cat gave birth to a litter of kittens on the guest room bed.

The Grahams, thinking this not to be the best arrangement, transferred them to a snugly-insulated box near the kitchen fireplace. But the cat – which evidently ruled the Graham household – preferred the spare room. Picking her kittens up one by one, she restored them once more to the guest room…. all excepting the last and smallest one, which was somehow left behind in the box.

The Grahams sat and watched. Eventually the tiniest kitten let out a minute sound – 'more of a squeak than a mew; it was almost a non-sound,' commented Ruth.

Instantly, soundlessly, the cat, *from* the guest room, bounded back into the kitchen, picked the kitten up and united it with the others. The cat had heard the sound – from three doors and two rooms away.

That, observed Ruth, describes the God who hears the feeblest of our prayers, 'our sighs, our tears and our murmurs'.

'Yea, He can feel breath when no voice can be heard for faintness'
(John Trapp, 1601–1669; vicar of Weston-on-Avon)

23

'I was sick and ye visited me'
(Matt. 25:36 KJV)

It was a welcome moment. There I was, still wobbly from the anaesthetic – and I could see my brother Michael and his wife Anros coming towards my bed. They were just in time.

'Michael – I'm going to be sick – could you get me a bowl?' My brother was all concern. 'Yes, yes – where do I find one?'

'At the far end. They're grey - like upturned hats.' Michael took off, grabbed a receptacle and headed back – only to hear from a nearby bed, 'Hey, what are you doing with my hat?!'

'No no,' explained Michael earnestly. 'I know it <u>looks</u> like a hat, but actually this is a receptacle to be sick into.'

'That is my hat!'

'Oh, okay, sorry.'

Somehow life brightens with episodes like that. No, you don't have to be rich or accomplished to be a visitor! But Jesus taught that at the last Judgment such apparently simple – and uncalculating – actions will help to provide a true identikit of the believer. How far do the deeds match the claimed beliefs?

'Inasmuch as ye have done it unto one of the least of these my brethren, ye have done it unto Me'
(Matt. 25:40 KJV)

24

*'But they that wait upon the Lord shall renew their strength;
they shall mount up with wings as eagles; they shall run and
not be weary; and they shall walk, and not faint'*
(Isa. 40:31 KJV)

Most people know what it is to 'wait'; the foot-tapping frustration, the checking of the watch! But God's Book tells us: *Don't JUST wait; Wait on the* LORD *– and He'll lift you!*

That was how the prophet Isaiah saw it for his own Jewish people after the exhausting experience of exile and subsequent restoration twenty-six centuries ago. How to become a real people again? It seemed that they were in an endless 'in-between' period, waiting for ever. *Not so,* came the message. *Bring God into it, and He will build you as a people.*

It's the Bible principle of 'creative waiting.' For most of life we are waiting for the next thing to happen; for news of the new baby, for the exam results, for the mortgage to come through! If we think that those boring, plodding periods are wasted, empty days, we may well spend a decade wishing our lives away. But it's what we do with those 'in-between' times that form us as the people we are meant to be. *Bring God into them.* Even in those 'empty' times, He is working! Let's believe it, and wait on Him, prayerfully, daily – and expect to come through.

*God is just as active five minutes before the break-through as he
is five minutes after*

25

'And the word of the Lord came to him:
"What are you doing here, Elijah?"'
(1 Kings 19:9)

Even the greatest of people have their moments of fragility, depression and panic. Here is Israel's greatest prophet, in flight from the wickedest woman of all time, Jezebel. Exhausted after travelling 300 miles south, from Jezreel, he spends a night in a cave at Mount Horeb. Actually, the original Hebrew of the Old Testament states that it was 'THE cave.'

That can only mean one thing! Why, it was the very same 'cleft' in the great rock where the Lord had hidden Moses centuries earlier (Exod. 33:21-23). *It was still there*, and Elijah takes refuge. What a place to be encouraged!

Then, standing outside once more, God's presence is made known to his servant. Through the powerful wind? No. By shaking the earth? No. Through a majestic fire, then? No, no... but in a still small voice.

He'll do that for you. Has there been a crisis? *Find a spot and make it your chapel.* Then trust God to speak to you. The Bible will help; try the psalms... and believe that the Lord will do for you what He did for Elijah – and get you going once more.

'When the storm passes over,
the grass will stand up again'
(Kikuyu proverb from East Africa)

26

'On the evening of that first day of the week, when the disciples
were together, with the doors locked for fear of the Jews, Jesus
came and stood among them, and said, "Peace be with you!"'
(John 20:19)

Yes, Sunday after the crucifixion; *not* an evening to show
a high profile. But now the reports of resurrection! True or
not?

Suddenly…He's there. No phantom; in a minute Jesus
would eat with them (Luke 24:42); here was a recognizable
body!

Peace be with you – it was a familiar blessing. Used by Jesus,
it had always been invested with divine power and authority.
Here now with the disciples was the one Man in history who,
by His own unique death and resurrection, has outfaced all the
fears and powers that threaten the peace of the human race.
This Easter blessing was the final clincher. 'Be at true peace!'
the Lord was saying. 'With me at your side nothing can ever
be lastingly bad again. *In life or death you are completely safe.*'

The disciples were 'overjoyed' – and so may you be, if you
are one of them! Are you shut in for the night now? Then,
whatever the happenings around you, receive the peace of
Christ – alive for evermore – upon yourself at this moment.

'The resurrection of Christ has altered the face of the universe'
(David Gooding)

27

'When he opened the seventh seal,
there was silence in heaven for about half an hour'
(Rev. 8:1)

Remember the quote in evening 4, 'God is the friend of silence'? Understandable if we've suffered from the all-night music of a nearby neighbour or the never-ending hubbub that throbs at the heart of any great city. But why is there silence at this point of John's vision in Revelation?

It is a dramatic interlude, between two series of mighty visions. And the silence is connected with 'the prayers of all the saints' (v. 3). *And 'saints' are simply believers.*

Never mind what noise may be surrounding you just now, or how insignificant your prayers may seem, as against the 'real' world of pop music and sports results. The indication is that heaven listens when the saints pray! Indeed, in John's vision, heaven itself goes silent, and the praises of the angels come to a halt. Even the great cosmic actions of God (v. 5) appear to be held back here – until the saints have prayed!

Does prayer have such power? It does. God has appointed prayer as the means by which we co-operate with His will. We pray; He works. Mentally shut off those outside sounds right now, and interlock with the very power of Heaven!

'Prayer is the pulse of life'
(Andrew Murray, 1828–1917)

28

'And will not God bring about justice for his chosen ones, who cry out to him day and night? Will he keep putting them off? I tell you, he will see that they get justice, and quickly.'
(Luke 18:7, 8)

In this parable of Jesus it was a clear enough picture; a widow, buffeted by injustice. With no money and no powerful friends, her only weapon lay in her non-stop appeals to the local judge. Not that he cared about her at all; it was only her refusal to stop bothering him that caused him to cave in!

God is not like the judge; that is Jesus' message here. And when afflicted people like the widow call upon their Lord for relief, the answer is instantaneous.

Do you face an issue, a falling-out with a callous individual or institution – even a religious group – right now? At any one moment, *day and night*, there it is once again, wrecking your peace and eroding your energies. Luke, in his writing, loves the theme of steady prayer. *God will not put us off,* whatever the time of night. Even if the final outworking of divine justice requires a necessary process (2 Pet. 3:9), our case will be 'quickly' taken up, there, in the very courts of heaven.

'Five words, a few broken sentences from a broken and contrite heart, are more desirable than to pray for hours without spiritual feeling'
(John Newton, 1725–1807)

29

'One thing is needful'
(Luke 10:42 KJV)

Marie Curie, the Polish-born French physicist and discoverer of radium, was asked in May 1910 by a reporter, 'If you could choose out of the whole world the one thing you would have, what would it be?'

The answer was, 'Just one gramme of radium! I can't buy it; radium is too dear for me.' It was an honourable answer from a woman who refused all financial profit from her discoveries.

Put that question into the context of all of life! *The one thing* – what would it be? Transport yourself to the home of Mary and Martha, near Jerusalem. Jesus, with His twelve disciples, has come in for a visit. Now He's speaking ... oh, such words! Mary sits, transfixed. Her sister meanwhile is frantically making thirteen Cornish pasties ... oh, the hassle! Finally she explodes. *Can't Mary help?* Our heart goes out to her.

But the big point is made by Jesus. 'Mary hath chosen that good *part*' (KJV). The word is ambiguous; it can mean 'portion'. What was the real dish of the day? Why – what it has to be for the whole of our lives; spiritually to be at the feet of Jesus, as a *disciple*, and – amid the many things that clutter every day – to be focusing on *the one thing*, the one loyalty and love, that injects integration and meaning into everything else.

Just now, at the end of your day, re-focus!

30

'Remember me with favour, O my God'
(Neh. 5:19)

Do they pray at British Cabinet Meetings in No. 10, Downing Street? They certainly need to! Here's one of many single-sentence 'arrow prayers,' of Nehemiah, appointed Governor of Judea in 432 BC. *The crises were many.* So pressed were he and his Jewish companions in the re-building of Jerusalem's shattered walls that they slept in their clothes (Neh. 4:23).

To pray ahead of time before the anticipated crisis - that nerve-jangling press conference, that terrifying union meeting or the dreaded health check – is to entrust the whole game-plan to God, who sees it in advance. Don't wait for the crunch-time to come! Get in front of the action *now* – with prayer.

Lord God, You know exactly the issues that are coming up in a few hours' time; you know the unforeseen surprises that may be sprung on me. May your Holy Spirit prepare the way now. Then, at the very point when the strategic moment arrives and crucial decisions are made – and You alone know when that will be – would you open the right mouth to speak, and block those opinions that do not accord with Your will. And at the precise moment that I step through the doorway of the coming situation, fill me with a glowing confidence that YOU are in charge.

The secret is to pray; then – however involved you are – mentally to step back ... and watch God do it!

31

'I will not give my glory unto another'
(Isa. 48:11 KJV)

How should you feel when a day has gone so successfully that, at its close, you feel a bit 'puffy'? So much done, such words of praise from every side! We are *grateful*, of course – for it is to the Creator Himself that we owe any success. But 'Success,' wrote John Venn two centuries ago, 'belongs to *God* – duty is *our* part!'

Success itself is a thing of the passing moment only, a fragile ally at the best of times. 'Nothing fails like success!' said Dean Inge of London, a century ago. Drink its heady potion, and the feeling wells up, *I did all that.* Pride can even hide itself in a cloak of false humility. What is the antidote to a sin that has wrecked so many characters?

Corrie Ten Boom, a heroic survivor of a World War II concentration camp, faced the same dilemma. Those who heard her inspired speaking in later years heaped praise upon her. Her remedy was to smile every time. 'Thank you!' she would say. 'Oh, *thank you!'* To Corrie, an affirmation was like being handed a beautiful flower. But then – on looking back at the end of the day – she would gather these words of praise into a single bouquet for Christ – 'These are for You!'

'When praise comes your way, don't inhale!'
(Dr Donald English at the Keswick Convention)

32

*'Don't be afraid ... Those who are with us are more than those
who are with them'*
(2 Kings 6:16)

At a particular period of intense insecurity in tropical Africa, Bishop Alexis Bilindagabo brought his church members up a hill for safety – and there preached and prayed with them.

Three messengers then arrived with the news that an armed company at the hill's base was coming to kill them. But the bishop remembered the story of Elisha, who – surrounded by enemies – assured his nervous companion that a far bigger *angelic* army was looking after them (2 Kings 6:8-17).

'Go down again!' said the bishop, 'and tell those people that this hill is surrounded by angels. Sure, they can come and kill us – but only if they can get past the angels!'

'We waited,' said Bishop Alexis. He then watched as the threatening army disbanded and melted away into the night.

It will not always happen with such results. But from time to time God lifts a corner of the curtain as a reminder that - *whatever happens* – an unseen angel host is on permanent duty.

*'No foes shall stay his might,
though he with giants fight'*
(John Bunyan, 1628–1688)

33

'And if I go and prepare a place for you, I will come again, and receive you unto myself; that where I am, there ye may be also'
(John 14:3 KJV)

'So what time were you up this morning?' I was about to broadcast *Thought for the Day* on BBC, and a young staff member was taking me to the studio. She answered, '4 a.m.'

'That's early!' I said. 'How do you get in here at that hour?'

'Easy!' she smiled. 'The BBC sends a car for me.'

That's the BBC for you, I reflected. Even for a junior staff member *there will be a conveyance*. Then, as a Christian, I thought of an infinitely more crucial journey – that begins with the death of a humble follower of Christ. When our time comes, must we struggle to make the journey into eternity alone?

Far from it. 'I will come again, and receive you unto myself", taught Jesus. Or better – as the original Greek has it – *'I am coming again.'* In ultimate terms, of course, this refers to the final return of Jesus at the end of history. But, once realize that – from Christ's Resurrection onwards – He is *always* 'the Coming One', you can rest assured, believer, that you are not on your own to make that final journey! None other than the risen Jesus will come in Person – and take you Home.

'At death you won't leave home – you'll go home'
(Pastor Rick Warren, California)

34

'The eternal God is your refuge,
and underneath are the everlasting arms'
(Deut. 33:27)

Here is Moses, shortly before climbing Mount Nebo, from where he could view with his own eyes the sweeping vista of the Promised Land into which his people would soon enter. They would have to enter without him, for he was about to die.

He blesses the tribes of Israel; and the final promise he imparts has given solace and assurance to millions who - like Moses - find themselves in the context of departure from this world. The words of verse 27 upheld my own wife, Liz, as her days on earth came to a peaceful close in a London hospice.

Those who experience bereavement will never forget it; the Long Day when you glance at your watch and cannot believe it is only eleven o'clock in the morning; why, it seems like four in the afternoon. Time has played tricks with your mind; too much has happened - the doctor, the phone calls, the rapid decisions, the churning emotions. *Let the promise hold us, when these days come upon us. Moses' reminder will be enough....*

> *If we could climb where Moses stood*
> *and fear that view no more,*
> *Not Jordan's stream, nor death's cold flood,*
> *would keep us from the shore.*

(Verse 6 of hymn: 'There is a Land of pure delight', by Isaac Watts)

35

'Precious in the sight of the Lord is the death of his saints'
(Ps. 116:15)

Precious?- after all that is said about death as 'the last enemy' – when we are confronted by such terms as *the snares of death... the sorrows of death... the dust of death*?

It is just about the biggest phenomenon of the Christian revelation – this dramatic change in perception! The seventeenth-century historian Richard Baker declared, 'To alter a thing from being vile to precious, is it not a greater miracle than to turn water into wine?'

I have taken many funeral services; hundreds of them. Often tragedy has struck; long illnesses may have prevailed; we weep and grieve over these loved ones we miss. But in the case of a Christian, along with the solemnity, there is inspiration as well. Such a funeral is a 'Gospel' occasion. *What has happened?*

Why, 'precious' believers are at last united with the Lord they always served, yet never saw – until now! Their redemption - that began at the Cross when they personally received Christ (John 1:12) – is now fully complete. God's assault upon the ravages of death has been achieved in yet another of His 'saints,' and *death is swallowed up in victory.* Truly safe at last!

'With Jesus ahead fear can go out by the back door'
(Cecil Bewes, missionary statesman, 1902–1993)

36

'Our friend Lazarus sleepeth; but I go,
that I may awake him out of sleep'
(John 11:11 KJV)

Yes, we owe this to the world's greatest Teacher, that we can bestow upon *death* – the worst of our adversaries – the kindest of descriptions: *sleep*.

Yet this raising of Lazarus – after four days in the tomb – was just the curtain-raiser! After all, Lazarus would die again one day and have to go through the whole process once more. No, it was *Christ's* Resurrection that was the real model for the future. That would be an historic event, giving a whole new dimension to the outlook and confidence of millions of us who, in our attachment to Jesus, fully expect to have resurrection bodies like His in the new heaven and the new earth.

The raising of Lazarus was just a taster! Christ's authority over death is stamped everywhere on this dramatic account in John chapter 11:

'Take away the stone!'
'Lazarus, come out!'
'Take off the grave clothes and let him go!'

Let's come under His rule now – and be Resurrection People!

'Thine be the glory – risen, conquering Son'

37

'Weeping may remain for a night,
but rejoicing comes in the morning'
(Ps. 30:5)

Bereavement: it's a little like the progress from a long night to a promising new day. Slowly, so slowly, the heavy darkness that is almost physical becomes imperceptibly grey, and the grey then begins to show tinges of pink, and ever so gradually you become aware that daylight is surrounding you once more.

Not that you are the same person ever again ... but – and it will be *others* who notice it about you – there will be a new depth to your life. It will be born of grief inevitably; yet instead of becoming more depleted as a person, it is possible that you will ultimately emerge stronger, not weaker; wiser, not embittered; outward-looking, not inwardly shrivelled. The loving support and steady prayers of others will do that for us. *Gradually!*

In Charlotte, North Carolina, it was a privilege to be at the graveside of Ruth Graham, wife of the well-known evangelist Billy Graham. All the family were gathered around. No big-time explanations were required; there was no need to ask the question 'Why?' In the context of the Gospel of Christ – whose interests Ruth had served all her life – *there was complete understanding.* I think we all emerged from the service richer, fuller – and deeply thankful for the risen Jesus, among us.

'Look up, bereaved! It won't be long – till Dawn!'

(Ruth Graham, *Sitting by my Laughing Fire*, World Wide Publications)

38

'Carry each other's burdens,
and in this way you will fulfil the law of Christ'
(Gal. 6:2)

'The law of Christ,' said Martin Luther, 'is the law of *love*.'

It is a tremendous thing to be 'carried' by the love and prayers of others. For there can be periods in life when our own prayers dry up completely; during a stay in hospital – when concentration is low - or during the crises of unemployment or bereavement. It is not that we have necessarily lost our faith; rather *we simply do not know what to say to God.*

When this happens we should be glad to let others do the praying on our behalf, and agree with the Lord that we will exist in a comfortable silence with Him, until such time as we begin to recover our equilibrium.

Particularly is this so in the case of bereavement, when distressing memories of a departing relative are at their most acute. *Time is needed.* Those images will not remain printed on the mind for ever. On the basis of human experience and the proven power of prayer, we can be assured that - given a few months – the old memories of loved ones, *when they were strong and well*, will increasingly infiltrate the screen of our minds. We don't have to work at it. And others can do the praying ...

'Lonely! The very word can start the tears…. Who walks with
Christ can never walk alone. He is here'
(English missionary in China; Gladys Aylwards 1902–1970)

39

*'For all things are yours, whether Paul or Apollos or Cephas
or the world or life or death or the present or the future, all are
yours: and you are Christ's; and Christ is God's'*
(1 Cor. 3:21-23 RSV)

On certain occasions in life you feel like a nobody. I remember being at a social function where there seemed to be important people all around me. There was even a former British Prime Minister in the room. How could I manage with these celebrities – even engage with them?

I thought, *I'll hand round the nuts.* Grabbing a couple of finger-bowls I started circulating. 'Won't you have a nut? Have a lot - have two!' It seemed to help ...

A Christ-centred mindset helps. Many of the apostle Paul's friends in Corinth would have been slaves. By belonging under powerful leaders they hoped for extra status. Paul thought differently. *On the contrary,* he insisted, *they belong to YOU!*

Why, in Christ all things belong to you. Indeed, Time, Eternity and the Future are all yours. And look at that vital phrase: 'Christ is God's' – He's not just one more leader. He's part of the very Godhead! Having Him in your life means that you know your way around; you have the freedom of the city!

Let that truth be a pillow for your head tonight

40

'Speak, Lord, for your servant is listening'
(1 Sam. 3:9)

It was around 1050 BC and Israel was at rock bottom. A demoralised priesthood, a hard people and an apparently silent God – could the land ever become alive again?

One night in Shiloh, Samuel - the child assistant to Eli the priest - was curled up in bed by the temple lamp. Then he heard a voice. *Was it Eli?* 'No,' insisted the old man. 'Lie down again.' Three times this happened. Eli then sensed that the call was divinely inspired. 'Lie down again,' he instructed, 'but the next time respond: *Speak Lord, for your servant is listening*. And see what happens!'

The rest is history. Samuel, who – we learn from the historian Josephus – was only twelve, had gone to bed as a pupil… *but by the time he opened Shiloh's temple doors the next morning, he was a prophet.* In that one night he discerned that through his future leadership Israel would find her soul again. The era of the prophets was about to begin, and the Bible – at long last – was to grow once more!

When the lamp of God seems to be extinguished in your family, your town, or your church, never assume that it cannot be re-lit. Hold on for this very thing to happen, and don't write off YOURSELF as the light-bearer – *whatever your age!*

Stay childlike, and your soul will never become hard

41

'Jesus was in the stern, sleeping on a cushion'
(Mark 4:38)

I once saw – and photographed on the beach – a first-century fishing boat that had just been excavated from the Sea of Galilee; 28 feet long - why, it could have been *that* very boat!

There were thirteen men in a boat that night. There's John, putting up the sail. There are Peter and James, giving a hand. *And who is that man in the stern?* 'Oh, don't you know? That's their leader, asleep; he's had an exhausting day.'

A terrifying storm boils up; the disciples are bailing for their lives... and Jesus sleeps on. They shake Him awake. 'Don't you know? Don't you care? We're going under!'

People have been asking that question ever since. Is heaven awake to what is happening in my life, in my family?

There on the lake, Jesus stills the elements – 'Peace! Peace, be still!' – and then looks at His friends. He's more concerned about *them* than He is about the storm! 'Where is your faith?'

Yes, He knows exactly what is going on. But don't be a 'fine-weather Christian', exercising trust only when the sun is shining. Who is that Man in the cockleshell of your own life? Get it right and you can ride the storms of any and every night.

'Christ's is the great voice of Hope in the world'
(Historian T.R. Glover)

42

'But he said to me, "My grace is sufficient for you,
for my power is made perfect in weakness"'
(2 Cor. 12:9)

This divine assurance to the apostle Paul, in all his weaknesses, encouraged American Fanny Crosby many years ago.

Afflicted by an eye infection when only a baby, she was given the wrong treatment by a doctor who placed hot poultices on her eyes. When the bandages were taken off, Fanny could see nothing beyond an impression of frosted glass. But her Puritan background and her godly grandmother enabled Fanny to grow up learning to 'see' all of life with her mind. She learnt Scripture. By the time she was ten she had memorised the first five books of the Bible, together with the four Gospels, the whole of the Psalms and plenty more. The rich theology in her soul was then poured into hymn writing. *Blessed Assurance, To God Be the Glory, He Hideth My Soul in the Cleft of the Rock* ... all in all she wrote over 7,000 hymns that have touched every continent. The Bible was her fuel, the Cross was her centre – and the Heart was her target!

When facing problems, let us not feel *undermined* by Fanny's story – if we feel we cannot rise to her level. Rather let us be *lifted* by the unique Bible principle of how God works!

'When you see the power of God in action, what you see is weakness'
(Dick Lucas of Bishopsgate, London)

43

The angel of the Lord encamps around those who fear him,
and he delivers them'
(Ps. 34:7)

Who is THE angel of the Lord (literally, 'the sent one')? Every time this figure features in the Old Testament Scriptures, it is clear that he is different from 'an angel,' such as Gabriel or Michael. Those angels are heavenly beings, yet they are created beings. They are not divine, and are not worshipped.

But if we read such passages as Genesis 22:11,12; Exodus 3:2-6 or Judges 2:1, it is evident that THE angel of the Lord speaks as God! Who is he? Why, he is the pre-incarnate second Person of the Trinity. Every time in the Old Testament that the Lord God manifests Himself visibly, He seems to do so in the Person that we today know as Jesus – who is from the very beginning.

To have the Lord Himself, then, 'encamping' around His true followers is a wonderful reassurance at times of trouble or uncertainty. To go to bed at night – knowing that (whatever may be happening) Christ Himself is vigilant for us, 'camping' watchfully over our interests – fills us with deep thankfulness. David the psalmist knew what it was to be 'delivered' from all that could make him afraid, and so can we.

'I will lie down and sleep in peace, for you alone,
O Lord, make me dwell in safety'
(David the Psalmist; Ps. 4:8)

44

'...night and day I constantly remember you'
(2 Tim. 1:3)

We wonder how we could ever emulate the apostle Paul in his constant 'remembering' of people in prayer. But prayer can indeed become a way of life – with certain tags to help us 'remember' others, whether on a bus or in bed; night or day!

Try praying on the fingers of one hand. Start with the THUMB. That's *closest* to you, so you remember relations, trusted friends and colleagues. The FOREFINGER next – used for pointing and directing – so you pray for those who have some authority over you; your teachers, your boss, your doctor, your church leaders.

Third comes the middle – the BIG FINGER. So you turn to the 'important' people; heads of state, members of government, ambassadors and local councillors. And because, to the believer, none are more 'important' than Christians in full-time mission (including overseas), these can be included too.

The fourth finger? Pianists call this the WEAK FINGER. That prompts us to remember the sick, the disadvantaged and refugee areas of this world. And last of all? Why, the LITTLE FINGER – that means 'little me,' with my needs, my requests and my own walk with God…. *You and I can do this anywhere.*

'Your words don't have to be eloquent, just earnest'
(Anne Graham Lotz, *I Saw the Lord*, Hodder)

45

'Don't bother me. The door is already locked, and my children are with me in bed. I can't get up and give you anything' (Luke 11:7)

My mother would act out Christ's parable for us as children, taking first the part of the man with unexpected visitors at midnight, then his visiting of the neighbour to borrow three loaves of bread. Next the persistent knocking:

Bang, bang.... 'Who is it?'
- 'It's only me; it's Fred! I need some bread right away. Three loaves should do it.'
- 'For goodness' sake, Fred! It's midnight – we're in bed!'
- *Bang, bang, bang.* 'Three loaves, my friend; *please?'*
- 'No, Fred, *No!* Call in the morning!'

Bang, bang, bang, bang, BANG. 'Just three little loaves?'

'What happened?' said Jesus. 'The man got his bread. Not for friendship, even – but because he never gave up.'

The point of the story is that God is utterly unlike the man in the story. God is not a lender but a giver. God never answers from inside a locked door. God never says 'Don't bother me.'

And, to God, it is never midnight

46

'Come unto me, all ye that labour and are heavy laden,
and I will give you rest'
(Matt. 11:28 KJV)

'Dear Sir,' wrote the twelve year old boy, 'Yesterday evening I gave my heart to Jesus, and this morning I feel as if tons and tons of lead had been lifted off my heart.'

'How do you feel right now?' A friend with an occult background had just broken with the past and received Christ. The reply was revealing. 'I feel lighter. I feel *pounds* lighter.'

A member of another belief-system described his conversion to Christ. 'I felt great weights were being lifted off me.'

It is the universal experience of millions, that Christ lifts the burdens of a lifetime caused by habit, prejudice, family break-up or alcoholism. The guilt attaching to them is gone and a new power is imparted by Christ's unseen Self, the indwelling Holy Spirit. We are not freed *from* future battles; rather we are set free *for* the fight for purity and a new way of life. The past is atoned for, the conscience is clear, the advantage in the immediate present is weighted in our favour. And tomorrow belongs to us! Chew on that as you rest in Christ tonight.

'Christ is the only Liberator whose liberation lasts for ever'
(Malcolm Muggeridge, Journalist and Broadcaster,
1903–1990)

47

*'I heard and my heart pounded, my lips quivered at the sound...
and my legs trembled. Yet I will wait patiently'*
(Hab. 3:16)

To the two armed superpowers of the seventh century BC (Assyria and Babylon), tiny Israel was just an outer-edge back-street suburb to where the *real* action lay! God's ancient people were shaking – *and so was Habakkuk, their prophet.*

The questions that Habakkuk posed to the Lord were the very questions that buffeted believers today might ask as we look at natural disasters, terrorist threats and crises affecting politics, the economy and the church itself. *Is God PARALYSED? Is God GOOD? Is God LATE? Will God WIN?* As an African pastor once phrased it, 'God, we know that you are in charge, but why don't you make it slightly more obvious!' Adversities on the personal front, too, can cause us to react along with the prophet, 'My legs trembled.'

But there's a kind of doubting that is okay! Habakkuk's brand was that of Doubt *within Commitment* – and it's expressed by the single word YET – that comes twice (v. 16, 18). He's going to hang on anyway! Despite the direst banner headlines, *believers know that they are in it for the long haul and that they will still be there at the very end.* Take heart (v. 19) and skip like a deer!

Glory, glory! Hallelujah! Our God is marching on!
(From the 'Battle Hymn of the Republic,' 1862, by
Julia Ward Howe)

48

'And they shall be mine, saith the Lord of hosts,
in that day when I make up my jewels'
(Mal. 3:17 KJV)

Here God encourages a tiny remnant of faithful believers, despite widespread spiritual apathy ... *you're my jewels!* Who are these godly people with their diamond-like qualities?

Rare people. You don't find sapphires and emeralds strewn around the kitchen; nor do you find Christ-like people cramming every street. But look hard, and you'll find them!

Beautiful people. They come in all ages and colours, and – as with sparkling jewels – we never want to let go of them! They attract us, not to themselves, but to Jesus, whom they resemble.

Valuable people. The Bible describes a godly wife as 'worth far more than rubies' (Prov. 31:10). 'Character is worth more than money,' said the evangelist D.L. Moody. History agrees!

Permanent people. Godly people – like hard-wearing diamonds that keep a watch ticking – are there in your street, in your hospital ward, your workplace. They are eternal to God.

Will we wake up tomorrow and exclaim, 'Wow, I've become holy!' No. *But becoming like Jesus is what we were born for.*

'Character is worth more than anything else in the whole world'
(D.L. Moody, 1837–1899)

49

'And such were some of you'
(1 Cor. 6:11 KJV)

The apostle Paul had listed some of the sins that characterised darkest Europe of the first century AD – including sexual perversions, theft and robbery, public disorder and alcohol abuse. 'And,' he comments to his Christian readers, 'many of you did those things – at one time!'

The assumption is that – once forgiven – spiritual resources enable us to battle with sins that once controlled us. We *can* win, despite Cicero's assertion, 'Mighty is the power of habit.'

The founder of a big British company was a new disciple of Christ, but alcohol was an old problem for him. Out walking one day, he saw a bar. Overwhelmed, he prayed. This was his 'prayer'. 'I'm very sorry, Lord; I've tried so hard – but just now I've *got* to have a double whisky.' He entered the pub.

'Yes, what will it be then?' asked the barman.

The new believer heard himself say, *'I'd like a lemonade please.'*

No doubt more battles lay ahead – but he was beginning to experience the power of Christ as unseen Companion!

'Be therefore continually prepared for contest'
(Thomas à Kempis of Germany, 1379–1471)

50

'Receive with meekness the engrafted word,
which is able to save your souls'
(James 1:21 KJV)

I heard a counsellor once say that his best 'prescription' for many of his clients suffering from depression was to meditate on some passage of Scripture before going to sleep.

'It's said that the last thing you think about before sleep stays with you throughout the night,' he declared. 'More than that – it can actually become a part of you, like a plant graft, affecting your mental and emotional outlook. To many of my clients I would say, "It's cumulative. Try it for the next thirty nights and see if your entire morale doesn't built up in an amazing way!"'

It's the simplest procedure imaginable. To glance through a psalm of David, and ask yourself, 'Is there anything here for me? That verse? Um, no. That bit, there? N-n-no. Ah! – THIS sentence; it's not even a whole verse, only a phrase, *but let it stay with me through the night.'*

And it will. Your head is on your pillow, the lights down ... and that sentence is turning around in your mind. You may not even completely understand it, but it's with you now – and the Spirit of God who inspired that word in the first place is doing His work in your soul as the night proceeds.

'Meditation is the soul's chewing'
(William Grimshaw, 1708–1763, vicar of Haworth, Yorkshire)

51

'As thy days, so shall thy strength be'
(Deut. 33:25 KJV)

I once asked the Ugandan revival leader, Festo Kivengere, how old he was. He didn't know. He could only reply, 'I was born during the rinderpest cattle plague in West Uganda.'

Perhaps an advantage of not knowing your age is that you can convince yourself for many years that you are perfectly all right for five sets of tennis ... until you find yourself puffing.

But need that matter anyway? Not for the believer! You may be a yard and a half away from where you ought to be on the court, but you are that much nearer to the winning post, nearer to those friends who have preceded you, nearer to a face-to-face encounter with Christ, whom you have worshipped and loved – but have never seen. You are going to see Him!

Here in our text is part of a blessing promised to the people of God shortly before Moses' death. The original Hebrew of this sentence is composed only of two words. It could be translated:

MORE DAYS MORE STRENGTH!

Fear not, Christian, if you are wearing bi-focal specs. By the power of God in your life, your best days are lying right ahead!

'He who believes preserves an eternal youth'
(*Fear and Trembling* (1843), Søren Kierkegaard)

52

'And the world passeth away and the lust thereof:
but he that doeth the will of God abideth for ever'
(1 John 2:17 KJV)

A middle-aged man called Augustine, aged fifty-six, staggered as he received the shocking news in Carthage that Rome – the capital of the civilised world – had been sacked by Barbarian hordes in a single day, August 24th, AD 410. Around Europe believing people were equally stunned. Their familiar world had fallen to pieces around them. Nothing stable was left.

But Augustine began to rally spirits everywhere as he took up his pen. His twenty-two-volume work, *The City of God*, took him some fifteen years to write – but it was to undergird the future culture of Europe for a thousand years. In it he contrasted the world's decaying cities with the eternal City of God, which continues for ever in his Church: *'Do not refuse to regain your youth in Christ, who says to you, "The world is passing away, the world is short of breath. Do not fear; thy youth shall be renewed as an eagle."'*

True Christianity has never folded in the face of a revolution, or at the collapse of an institution. It has witnessed such things often enough – and possesses the spiritual resources to rebuild. *What were the newspaper headlines today?* Learn to read them through the lens of history – and of faith!

'Christianity stabilizes society without sterilizing it'
(Historian T.R. Glover)

53

'When you lie down, you will not be afraid;
when you lie down, your sleep will be sweet'
(Prov. 3:24)

Years ago there was a leading English tennis player called 'Bunny' Austin. Of him it was said that if his day had been disturbed by some unresolved issue, he would go onto court unable to give of his best, and even the slightest bad call could unnerve him. However, if he began a match thoroughly settled, having had a massage and with his mind rested and at ease, no amount of unwelcome incidents on court could interfere with his play – and he could out-perform the world's best.

A Christian's soul is like the body of a highly-tuned sports star. Every day is *an event*. We may not be found on an athletics track or tennis court – *but, one way or another, tomorrow will find us as servants in the courts of the Lord God Almighty.*

Better, then, to emerge to a new day having had a night of *'sweet sleep.'* But that takes some *preparation;* regular hours, discipline over night-time TV viewing, nothing between you and your Maker, a prayer as you go to sleep. An exacting programme would be expected by any top athlete. And the service of Jesus Christ tomorrow deserves our best! So let us now wish each other an easy mind and a restful *Goodnight....*

'A day in thy courts is better than a thousand elsewhere'
(Ps. 84:10)

54

'Why troublest thou the Master any further?'
(Mark 5:35 KJV)

There was plenty to discourage ordinary people from coming to Jesus - especially non-Jews, lone women, outcasts, children or hopeless cases. But, secretly or publicly, still they came.

Can anyone come?
Someone once said to me, 'After neglecting Jesus for years, I haven't got the nerve to come to him.' But take heart from the many in the Gospel stories who *did* come - and were rewarded.

Will anything happen?
Again, take heart! Jesus was no dispenser of mere *advice.* In every experience – success, guilt, anxiety, aimlessness or sorrow – Christ will meet us at our heartfelt points of need.

Has anything changed?
Certainly. With the dimension having *expanded* from the local to the universal and from the temporal to the eternal, the Spirit of Jesus now meets with seeking people on every continent. *Does that include you?* Tell him your needs this very evening.

'I found in Christ the full supply of my every need'
(Sir James Simpson, discoverer of Chloroform, 1811–1870)

55

*'I have seen all the things that are done under the sun;
all of them are meaningless, a chasing after the wind'*
(Eccles. 1:14)

Ecclesiastes, 'the Preacher,' was at the very least a writer in the tradition of King Solomon, and was most likely Solomon himself (ch. 1, v. 1). He must have lain on his bed as he contemplated his very full life – and then deliberately put himself in the position of atheist. *His conclusion:* If you take God out of the frame, nothing makes sense.

He tells us in chapter 2 that he had tried everything in his time! The *sensual* (vv.1-3), the *cultural* (vv. 4-7), the *material* (v. 8) and the *powerful* (vv. 9, 10) – none of it brought satisfaction.

The book of Ecclesiastes is there to pull us up short and make us ask, Is there more to the one-dimensional life of sleep, rise, eat, work, eat, work, watch, sleep, rise – and then at death getting our name into the local papers for just one more time?

The Preacher adopts the stance of the unbeliever, pushing him along the line of his own logic. *Is this what you were born for?* In rare glimpses, Ecclesiastes reveals himself in his true colours and gives the tiniest of hints that there *is* an answer to the meaning of life. It consists in knowing the one true God.

*'Fear not that your life shall come to an end,
but rather fear that it shall never have a beginning'*
(John Henry Newman, 1801–1890)

56

*God's plan... 'to bring all things in heaven and on earth
together under one head, even Christ'*
(Eph. 1:10)

The key to life's meaning lies right here. First, through the created order, God's power and nature are revealed – in what Bible students call His *general revelation*. How else could the God-consciousness of millions of people have come about, even in a world flawed by human sin? But there's more.

Throughout the Old Testament and into the New, God's *special revelation* was given – through acts of deliverance, through inspired messengers and prophets, and supremely in the coming of Jesus, long foretold and now crowned as universal Lord and Saviour and Head of all things.

Some ask, 'I can understand the concept of "God", but where does Jesus *fit in*?' It was an Egyptian theologian, Athanasius, who gave the answer sixteen centuries ago: *'The only system of thought into which Jesus Christ will fit is the one in which he is the starting point.'* He is the source – and goal – of everything.

Get that wrong, and we will be like the man doing up his shirt buttons, *starting with the wrong button*. It will end in a muddle! Get *Christ* wrong – and existence itself won't make sense.

'Follow Him in life and you will follow Him in eternity'
(K.P. Yohannan of Gospel for Asia, *Touching Godliness*, GFA Books)

57

'But when the time had fully come, God sent his Son'
(Gal. 4:4)

So how would we *describe* a Christian world-view? Imagine that I am creating a raft with which to negotiate the rocks and currents of modern thought. Out of its centre is a mast. Its flag bears the name *Jesus Christ.* He must be central. He is for ever!

Bible history is shaped like an hourglass, wide at the top and bottom and with a narrow centre – through which pass the tiny grains of sand. The top is massively wide: *'Let us make man!'*

But soon the glass narrows down – to the middle east, and to a nation called Israel – selected to be a light to the world. But it fails in its calling, and under God's judgment four-fifths of its people are carried off into captivity. The narrowing continues when the remaining one fifth also is taken – and the end of the Old Testament leaves us with a tiny faithful remnant.

Into the New Testament. We are now down to twelve men and their leader. One turns traitor, another turns coward, and the rest are scattered … leaving a solitary grain at the centre. At that point He *is* 'Israel'. By Christ's death and resurrection, all God's saving plans for the world are fulfilled – in one Man!

But from there the widening process begins, as his followers proclaim Christ in Jerusalem, Judea, Samaria … the world!

At the centre of a Christian world-view is Christ

58

'You alone are the Lord. You made the heavens, even the highest heavens and all their starry host, the earth and all that is on it, the seas and all that is in them'
(Neh. 9:6)

I was once criticised at a party about my beliefs. I conceded that I had much to learn, but then I challenged my critic - 'Describe to me your own world-view.' He hesitated. 'I haven't got one.' 'Oh but you have!' I said. 'The smallest child has *some* perceptions about life. So what do *you* believe?'

'Well, I'm an atheist.' *'Come on!'* I continued. 'I'm not asking you what you *don't* believe, but what you *do* believe – about life here!' Suddenly my friend was struggling – but I'd only asked him two questions.

Take the imaginary 'raft' that I've assembled in my mind as a credible world-view. At its centre is Jesus Christ, who alone can interpret life for us. But then my raft needs some undergirding planks. And they consist of four mighty truths.

I've just space for the first! *Creation* tells us that we are not a collection of biochemical reactions, but that behind everything is a Creator – and that I am made in His image. Build on that truth and you'll have insights into your own origin, humanity, sport, wealth-creation, sex, architecture, art and conservation!

'Whoever made this Book made me!'
(A Chinese reader of The Bible)

59

'There is no-one who does good, not even one'
(Ps. 14:3)

If a Christian's world-view resembles a raft, composed of four great planks, the second plank – after that of Creation – is what theologians call The Fall. *It explains so much!* Human sin goes back to our earliest ancestors - in their bid to act independently from the Creator (Gen. 3).

We have all been affected ever since, in that Adam and Eve were not simply human beings, but 'prototype' humans – *representatives and leaders* of the whole human race. They were not puppets programmed to be good, but free agents. They fell, and we all fell with them. If a jelly mould becomes dented, every jelly from then on will carry that dent. So with The Fall.

The Fall then is not God's fault. Augustine wrote, 'The cause of evil is not the good, but defection from the good.'

No part of us is free from this taint. The Fall even affects creation - for we were supposed to be its custodians. This second plank is vital to our understanding of humanity and its problems, murder, promiscuity, wars, disasters and death; we lament these things and combat them, *but we are not shocked.* Is there a remedy for human sin? There is – we work on and pray on ... in the awareness of a Third Plank!

'The most remarkable thing about wrongdoing is that it is universal'
(Bishop Stephen Neill, 1900–1984)

60

'...the Lamb slain from the foundation of the world'
(Rev. 13:8 KJV)

The theme of *Redemption*, centering in the Cross, is the third plank of our 'raft.' Even at the time of The Fall, Jesus' death on The Cross and the victory stemming from Calvary was divinely predicted to the serpent: *And I will put enmity between thee and the woman, and between thy seed and her seed; it shall bruise thy head, and thou shalt bruise his heel* (Gen. 3:15 KJV).

The announcement was no more than a tiny bubbling spring, in the face of our human disaster. But it would broaden out into the mighty river of Redemption, sweeping through the entire Bible message. It would reach its destination when Jesus Christ, very God of very God - but also the descended human 'seed' of the woman - would be 'bruised' for our sins, and this by the will of the Lord God (Isa. 53: 5 and 10).

The Cross was also the occasion of the 'bruising' of Satan's *head*, so ensuring the ultimate overthrow of evil. Romans 16:20 tells us that even the newest believers, saved from their sins, are now able to crush Satan under their feet!

This third 'plank' assures us of victory over death, and that no one at all is beyond the redeeming, forgiving power of the Lamb of God, whose saving intervention divides our history.

Evil overcome, sins forgiven, death conquered, Heaven opened!

61

'They will see the Son of Man coming on the clouds of the sky,
with power and great glory'
(Matt. 24:30)

The Bible has had many pre-runs of 'The Day of the Lord.' Noah's flood, the locust invasion of Joel's time, the overthrow of wicked Babylon; these and other upheavals were but pointers to the final 'day of our Lord Jesus Christ' (1 Cor. 1:8). *Here is the fourth plank that makes up the raft of Christian understanding about our existence.*

History is not circular or locked into an unending stalemate. Rather, everything is leading to *a Conclusion*, to the new heaven and the new earth that will be inaugurated at the second Coming of Jesus Christ. His return will establish the final triumph of the kingdom of God and will usher in the last Judgment, so bringing about the dismantling of the whole empire of Satan that has so harassed us across the centuries.

The Cross and Resurrection secured the victory over evil. Christ's return will make it final! Believers echo Paul's words in 1 Thessalonians 4:17 – 'And so we will be with the Lord for ever.' *A strong view of the future energizes us in the present!*

Four planks: Creation, the Fall, Redemption and the final Triumph: Build a mature world-view that stands every test!

Christians are to be childlike, but never childish

62

'But the saints of the Most High shall receive the kingdom,
and possess the kingdom for ever, for ever and ever'
(Dan. 7:18 RSV)

You could not imagine a more discouraging setting in which to make such a gigantic claim. Here is Daniel, an exile along with thousands of his fellow Jews, in mighty, heathen Babylon. And yet, lying on his bed, many years into his ordeal, he receives a God-given vision of the Son of Man in irradiated splendour, whose dominion would outlast every empire unleashed upon the world. Daniel 7 unlocks for us the whole vast panorama.

THE SHAPE OF HISTORY. Successive world powers – portrayed here as monsters – have no permanence at all. Yet in the teeth of opposition, the kingdom of God advances. It is the *only* body that survives to the very end of civilisation!

THE RULE OF GOD. Here we see God's unshakable throne. And what is 'the kingdom'? It is the rule of God, through the chosen King, Jesus (*the Son of Man*), in the lives of His subjects world-wide. Know the King – and you possess the kingdom!

THE COMING OF CHRIST. Visions of Christ's glory occur elsewhere (Ezek. 1:25-28; Luke 9:28-36; Acts 7:55, 56; Rev. 1:12-16). He came as a Child at Bethlehem, but read Daniel 7 and you have the *full* picture of the Son of Man!

'We are all working for the great kingdom of God'
(Eric Liddell, missionary and Olympic gold medallist,
1902–1945)

63

'I left Trophimus sick in Miletus'
(2 Tim. 4:20)

Who was Trophimus, and how did he get his name into the Bible? A Greek citizen from Ephesus, he had become a friend and associate of the apostle Paul. At one point their adventures had provoked a city-wide riot in Jerusalem (Acts 21:27). Now the adventures of Trophimus have left him sick at Miletus. Paul had left him there, presumably on his journey west. But now Paul is in prison at Rome, awaiting death.

What do you do, when a valued friend is in need, eight hundred miles away – and you can do nothing? One answer is that you tell a friend who *is* close to the scene. That friend was Timothy, to whom this letter of Paul's is addressed – and Timothy, like Trophimus, was a citizen of Ephesus, and only thirty miles away. We can be sure that Timothy took action!

I remember one of my very best friends, Roger Salisbury, coming to see me once in hospital. 'Don't go, Roger!' I begged as a Chinese nurse held the sick-bowl for me. 'I won't go,' he promised. His visit made my day. There is such a thing as the Christian grapevine, a fellowship of prayer and trust – that today is world-wide. You read of a disaster somewhere – and your thoughts and prayers fly to your far-away friends. Do you have such friends? List them. Send emails. And pray!

'A little faith and a great God are enough'
(Alfred Stanway, Australian missionary statesman, 1908–1989)

64

'When I lie down, I say, When shall I arise,
and the night be gone?'
(Job 7:4 KJV)

For suffering Job, nights seemed endless, and I know the feeling. But for some, a long night is no big deal. As she entered widowhood my grandmother, Evelyn Bewes, didn't bother too much about bed. She would come and stay with us, and my Dad would bring her early morning tea at 6 a.m. *She would still be writing letters.* Then she would have her tea and her time of quiet with God. By eight o'clock she would be at breakfast!

Some people *can* live like that – and they need not feel guilty, despite the many virtuous epigrams drilled into them:
Early to bed and early to rise
Makes a man healthy, wealthy and wise.

Such a sentence might well have come from one of Job's useless 'comforters'! True, night-time and sleep are supposed to coincide, but if this is not happening and you are one such 'sufferer', you are in good company. What to do? Knock off some emails? Hang on to that Scripture memory verse? Make yourself tea? Pray? There is a well-worn adage that still has plenty of value: *Don't lie and count sheep; talk to the Shepherd.*

But equally, there is no harm in emulating the disciplinarians!

'I have so much to do that I must go to bed'
(Georges Henri Lemaitre, clergyman and astrophysicist,
1894–1966)

65

'Ye sold me.... God sent me'
(Gen. 45:5, 7 KJV)

How encouraged I was to hear my friend, Roger Salisbury, preaching on this topic of God's providence. *Think of it!* How did Joseph feel on being thrown into a pit by his brothers, the other 'children of Israel' – only later to be sold to merchants bound for Egypt? Further trials followed when – in household service in Egypt – he was unjustly jailed. Yet Joseph trusted that God was somehow present in every fresh setback, to bless him - and others too.

He rose to prominence in the land. The epic ends with his once-estranged brothers reconciled, and settled with him in Egypt. From there, four hundred years later under Moses, the entire story of world redemption was to begin! It is the old story of a mess of tangles on the reverse side of the carpet – *'You sold me'* – but see the other side, and a pattern is there – *'God sent me!'*

What is happening to you at this moment? Believe that God is at work in your life! 'Oh,' we say, 'But there in Genesis we're reading about the Children of *Israel* – they're special!' Not really. *They were one of the most dysfunctional families going.* But from them God was going to create 'the twelve tribes of Israel'. One day they would feature, with the twelve apostles, among the four and twenty elders in the Book of Revelation!

The world which clouds thy soul with doubt
Is but a carpet inside out'
(Hannah More, Christian reformer and writer, 1745–1833)

66

'Moses drew near to the thick darkness where God was'
(Exod. 20:21 ESV)

Something held the Children of Israel back when they saw Moses approaching Mount Sinai at God's command. True, they had received deliverance from Egypt, food from heaven, and water from the rock. But they were fearful of anything that brought them up against the unknown (v. 18).

Yet at the heart of the unknown was the God who would lead them to the Promised Land. Moses entered the darkness alone.

From time to time an individual, a family, a nation will face a dark, uncertain future. Shortly after World War II had broken out in 1939, the King of England, George VI, was due to give his Christmas broadcast. Earlier, the Queen had handed him the words of a poem, written by an American, Minnie Louise Haskins, in 1908. The King quoted from it in his final words. Listeners never forgot it. It went around the world. It still provides inspiration to anyone facing the unknown:

'I said to the man who stood at the Gate of the Year, "Give me a light that I may tread safely into the unknown." And he replied, "Go out into the darkness, and put your hand into the Hand of God. That shall be better than light, and safer than a known way."'

67

'Through many tribulations we must enter
the kingdom of God'
(Acts 14:22 RSV)

Rejected at Antioch, threatened in Iconium, stoned at Lystra, frustrated in Bithynia, flogged in Philippi, hounded in Thessalonica, ridiculed in Athens, harassed in Ephesus, arrested in Jerusalem, tried in Caesarea, shipwrecked at Malta, imprisoned in Rome.... Friends, when it came to 'tribulation' the apostle Paul could say, *Been there, done that!*

And he was our top Christian spokesman of all time. No limousine at Damascus – he left over the city wall in a basket!

It was shortly after being thought dead at Lystra that he recovered and took on Lystra yet *again*, accompanied by Barnabas. And this was their main message – that Christians can *expect* trials and 'tribulations'. They do not lead to a dead end, but are part of the anticipated road that leads us through to glory (1 Pet. 4:12, 13)! The disciple of a Leader who has so suffered must be prepared to travel the same road.

From nursery school through to old age, the follower of Jesus is not promised an easy path. And yet, and yet! Once we have been drawn to Christ, we would not choose any other path.

'Eighty and six years have I served Him and He hath done me
no wrong; how then can I blaspheme my King who saved me?'
(Bishop Polycarp's refusal to deny Christ.
Martyred Feb. 22nd, AD 156)

68

'God has chosen to make known among the Gentiles the glorious riches of this mystery, which is Christ in you, the hope of glory'
(Col. 1:27)

Liz and I were at the 'Wimbledon' of art, the Uffizi Gallery in Florence. Suddenly, there before us were the Michelangelo sculptures! I had read avidly about them, but had never seen any of them. The unfinished ones were as fascinating as the rest – for we could see how, by chiselling patiently away, the artist was 'releasing' a figure which, *in his mind*, was already present in the block of marble, and only needed to be set free.

This is what is happening to the Christian. Willingness and co-operation are necessary on our part, but the Creator knows exactly what He wishes to produce in us, for He has a model right by his side. Elijah? Daniel? Luke or Barnabas? A Wesley? A Hannah More? No, the model is *Jesus Christ*, and the aim is to produce a figure who, in character, resembles HIM. *Christ in you*: that is the objective!

Those readers of Colossians 1:27 must have said, *It can't happen; look at me! I'm a Gentile ... I have an alcohol problem ... I was involved in an affair ... I'm too old and ill to start now ... I'm just a useless block.* But – frequently through sufferings and lessons bitterly learnt – the process continues, of steadily chipping, chipping away. Something beautiful is to emerge!

'Never, never be content if your soul does not grow'
(*Holiness*, by Bishop J.C. Ryle of Liverpool, 1816–1900)

69

'He is able to save completely those who come to God through him, because he always lives to intercede for them'
(Heb. 7:25)

My American friend was coming through England for the first time – for one day only. I asked him, 'What would you like to do? I'll look after you!' The reply was immediate.

'Even more than seeing the Crown Jewels, I would like to see the Centre Court at Wimbledon's Tennis.'

'Leave it to me,' I replied, *'I know a man!'* The man was a top tennis official, and he got us in – out of hours – and we saw everything. We even stuffed grass cuttings from the famous turf into our pockets. My friend was ecstatic… .

But every Christian can say *I know a Man!* He is Jesus Christ, and – being who He is – He has the power to usher even the newest one of His followers to the 'centre' of the universe itself; to the very courts of heaven, God's dwelling place. This is what is meant by His *intercession* for us. It is not exactly that Jesus is kneeling at the Throne, pouring out a stream of petitions, but rather that He is there as the Friend we know, *supporting our case as we come in prayer.*

'Can God the Father turn a deaf ear to his own Son?'
(Joni Eareckson Tada, *When God Weeps*, Zondervan)

70

'By day the Lord directs his love, at night his song is with me –
a prayer to the God of my life'
(Ps. 42:8)

This is a psalm of swirling currents. The emotions alternate between desperation, tears, wistful memories and inner disturbance. Why is my soul downcast? Has God forgotten me? Are my critics right when they tauntingly ask where my God is? Although it is not stated that this was a psalm of David, the words certainly read like his roughest experiences.

Be glad that those sentiments are there. It is just as 'spiritual' to groan in God's presence as it is to grin; the psalms have room for both sighs and songs, weeping and praising. Here, even amid the psalmist's depression, a 'song' element is indeed present at our verse 8. It highlights the believer's underlying conviction that nowhere in a twenty-four hour period can it be said that God's hands are off the tiller and that all singing is banned! We have Paul and Silas bleeding as prisoners, singing in the stocks at midnight, to prove the point (Acts 16:25).

The encouragement is from the *Lord,* however; even the song is 'his song.' For ourselves, we may find no words to say, but we will find comfort in Christ's love that covers us in every predicament. We may turn over and rest - secure in that abiding love.

'Love, with its overloading, short-circuits prayer'
(From the personal prayer journal of Ruth Bell Graham)

71

'A cloud as small as a man's hand is rising from the sea'
(1 Kings 18:44)

Through Elijah – the most colourful of all Israel's prophets – a judgment of three and a half years' drought had been pronounced upon the land. Now the dry spell was due to end.

The valley of Jezreel was shimmering in the sun. But – 'It's going to *rain*,' Elijah assures King Ahab. He begins to pray.

At last he looks up. 'What's the weather doing?' The lookout stares westwards. 'It's a beautiful day out there!' Elijah prays steadily on. *Friends, when the skies are like brass we also must be prayerfully alert for the tiniest signals that GOD is at work!*

A seventh time the aide reports back – 'Nothing yet – except a microscopic cloud.' It's enough for Elijah. 'Tell Ahab, "Hitch up your chariot and *ride* – before the rain stops you!"' The skies go black, and it starts to pour. See Elijah, caught up in the excitement, running ahead of Ahab, on the seventeen-mile stretch to Jezreel, in the drenching, refreshing rain of God!

No, there was nothing special about Elijah. James 5:17 says he was just one of us. *Let's be involved ourselves then – in prayer!*

'Expect great things from God;
Attempt great things for God'
(William Carey, missionary to India, 1761–1834)

72

'Their works do follow them'
(Rev. 14:13 KJV)

'I'm a nobody,' someone may be saying at the end of a day. 'I'm just a humble primary school teacher ... a nurse ... an unknown missionary.' *Yet you are touching precious lives every day.* No one, for example, ever forgets their first teacher!

We had an adored missionary 'aunt,' Lorna Bowden, back in Kenya days. 'Aunty Lorna,' recalled my brother Peter, 'was the most beautiful person I had ever seen.' She became my sister Elizabeth's godmother. A single woman of uncertain age and medically unqualified, it was nevertheless understood that she was the only one around who could do injections.

'I do hope I can get this injection right, Sylvia,' murmured Lorna anxiously to my mother one day. She held up the syringe to the light. 'I can't see any bubbles. Ready?'

'Yes, yes, Lorna; do get on with it!'

'Very well ... er ... here goes then. Oh dear, let's just have a little word of prayer!' By the end, both women were in tears.

She never knew it, but Aunty Lorna's life of love was indelibly stamped on us for ever. 'Saints' like her are never forgotten – least of all by God – and nor are we, if it is Him we are serving.

'What women these Christians have!'
(Libanius, teacher in Rhetoric to
preacher John Chrysostom, AD 314–393)

73

'He has also set eternity in the hearts of men'
(Eccles. 3:11)

Although the book of Ecclesiastes deliberately adopts the viewpoint of atheism – to demonstrate its emptiness – it drops just enough hints to remind us of the eternal dimension to life!

Arthur Stace of Sydney, Australia, was a *human* reminder – to an entire city. A drunken down-and-out, he wandered into St Barnabas Church, Broadway, one night, and there he was led to faith. One day in church, the preacher cried, 'Oh, if only the word ETERNITY could be written across this city of Sydney!'

Arthur thought to himself, *I'll do that.* He took some chalk that night and wrote on a pavement the word *ETERNITY* in beautiful copperplate – then again ... and again. Nightly he wrote the one-word sermon – sometimes fifty times in an evening – on walls and sidewalks. People wondered who the nocturnal artist was. *The secret finally blew after twenty-five years,* and Arthur became 'Mr Eternity.' He died in the 1960s.

Years later, on Millennium eve, December 31st 1999, Sydney's Harbour Bridge was lit up with a brilliant display of fireworks. Then, as the glow subsided, eight gigantic letters in the familiar copperplate remained in neon lights, ninety feet high across the bridge ... ETERNITY. It was a city's tribute to the down-and-out of decades earlier. Arthur Stace has never been forgotten.

'God hath chosen the weak things of the world'
(1 Cor. 1:27 KJV)

74

'You have been given fulness in Christ'
(Col. 2:10)

Years ago when Bible knowledge was at a low ebb, it was held that there were three classes of people: *sinners, penitents* and *saints*. Today we can fall into a similar error – in thinking of the *un-converted*, the *converted* and *'super-Christians'*! But the Scriptures only teach of two classes, *believers and unbelievers*. By addressing 'the saints,' then, the apostle Paul meant all Christian *believers* – even the lowly despised slaves.

Take it in. The most inexperienced disciple is united with Jesus from Day One – and has 'fulness' in Him. But are we in Him, or is He in us? Throw a sponge into the bath.... Is the water in the sponge or is the sponge in the water? *Both are true!*

'Fulness....' The King James Version translates the verse 'complete in Him.' In the Greek, the phrase carries the idea of a ship, fully rigged, *complete* with all that is necessary for the voyage. Nothing more has to be added – we can sail! This was the point that Paul needed to get across to his readers. Union with Christ is *completeness*, he urged; never be fooled by false teachers who offer extra 'power' or special insider-knowledge (Col. 2:8, 16-23). Of course *we* have more to *learn!* But in union with Him we are equipped from Day One...

Have faith in Christ and you are ready for anything,
thankful for everything, afraid of nothing
(C.H. Spurgeon, 1834–1892)

75

'You died with Christ'
(Col. 2:20)

Being united with Jesus incorporates His followers into every stage of His saving work. You say, 'I can't believe that' – but you can! Think of a thread that has been attached to a needle. Wherever the needle goes, the thread follows. The process is the same with those who are attached to Christ by faith; they are united with Him for ever. *He died, so we 'die.' He was raised; we are raised. He ascended; we ascend with Him. He will appear at His final Return; we shall appear with Him!*

Take this first of the four occurrences of 'With Christ' in Colossians 2 and 3 – 'You *died* with Christ.' The principle goes back to the Old Testament book of Leviticus. A wrongdoer would bring a sacrificial animal and – laying his hand upon its head – would confess his sin. The animal would symbolically bear the transgressor's sin. When it died, the wrongdoer symbolically 'died' with it, and the sin was pardoned.

Are you repelled by that concept? *You should be.* We should tremble at the idea of another dying in our place. The fulfilment of all this was in Jesus, *the Lamb of God.* When we first trust in Christ's atoning death for our sins, we too 'die' *with Him.* Pardon is complete – and we become enemies of sin.

'My faith would lay her hand on that dear head of Thine'
(From a hymn by Isaac Watts, 1674–1748)

76

'You have been raised with Christ'
(Col. 3:1)

If the first occurrence of the phrase 'with Christ' concerned the believer's *dying* with Jesus, the second concerns his resurrection with Him…and look at the language! *You have BEEN raised with Christ.* There is, certainly, a day in the future when actual bodies will be raised from the grave, free from all decay and pain - remember the image of the thread following the needle? But the assurance of Colossians 3:1 is that the resurrection life has already started!

Implication: Those raised with Christ will start to *live* that way – and it is a supernatural way. When it happens, society takes notice. The fourth-century Roman emperor Julian ascribed Christianity's remarkable growth in the first three centuries to the kindness that Christians showed to strangers.

Don't you need a badge to indicate your faith? Distinctive clothing, a special head-covering? Is devotion to a special region, city, language or shrine a desirable requirement for the believer in Jesus Christ? No, none of that. Your give-away credentials – wherever you come from – will lie in your entire attitude and bearing, your speech, your smile. These things will say, *Someone has come into my life – and lifted me upwards.*

'You must not only seek heaven;
you must also think heaven'
(J.B. Lightfoot, English theologian, 1828–1889)

77

'Your life is now hidden with Christ in God'
(Col. 3:3)

Here is a *third* 'With Christ' of Colossians 2 and 3. Followers of Christ – like the thread following the needle – are said to have *died* with Christ and been *raised* with Christ. But in addition to being identified with His death and resurrection, we are also incorporated into His ASCENSION.

For that is what is meant by our being hidden with Christ. With His saving work completed, Jesus ascended to heaven. There He was hidden from the eyes of the world as He took up His triumphant rule. *And we too are hidden with Him.* True, others can see our bodies – but an essential part of us is now hidden from view, as we live in the intimacy of an unseen relationship with Christ, our best Friend! Paul even says that we now *sit* with Christ in the heavenly places (Eph. 2:6).

Hidden, with Christ, in God. A preacher once said, 'Take a hymn sheet – it represents *you.* Place this frail thing inside a hymn book – it represents *Christ.* Now place the hymn book inside a Bible – this represents *God.* Look' – said the preacher, 'Your life is hidden with Christ in God. Nothing can touch your life unless it comes through God and through Christ. Even the devil can't harm you!' On that note, *Goodnight!*

'How important it is that we should cultivate the hidden life'
(Guy H. King, Vicar of Christ Church, Beckenham
from 1935–1956)

78

'You also will appear with Him in glory'
(Col. 3:4)

Someone was asking a small boy about a forthcoming event:
- 'Are you going to be at the Pageant?'
- 'Well actually,' came the reply, 'I'm going to be *in it!'*

There is all the difference of Eternity between *witnessing* the final glory of Christ's triumphant return to this world and *participating* in it. The present hiddenness of the ascended Christ will one day be ended in the full blaze of His 'appearing' – and every eye will see Him (Rev. 1:7). But not all will *appear with Him* in the event that is to usher in the new heaven and the new earth. This makes logical sense; it would be strange if someone who had nothing to do with Christ in this life expected to have everything to do with Him in the next.

This fourth occurrence of the *with Christ* phrase represents the only one of the Lord's saving actions that has yet to take place. The prospect of involvement in Christ's return should mould the direction in life of every one of His active followers.

'I do not think that in the last forty years I have lived one conscious hour that was not influenced by the thought of our Lord's Return'
(Parliamentary reformer Ashley Cooper,
Earl of Shaftesbury, 1801-1885)

79

'So shall we bear the likeness of the man from heaven'
(1 Cor. 15:49)

In this great 'resurrection' chapter of the Bible, believers in Christ learn that - although at present we bear in ourselves the image of fallen, earthly Adam – in the next life we shall bear the likeness of the risen Christ! Indeed, we are expected even now to begin bearing His likeness in our daily living. In the Greek text, 'likeness' is *eikona* – from which we have our modern word 'icon.' Replicas of Jesus! Will that really be us?

A Christian leader who had known the apostle John was Ignatius, who died as a martyr under the rule of the Roman emperor Trajan, around the year AD 107. Ignatius was so concerned to carry his Lord with him into his every action, that those who knew him gave him a nickname, *The Godbearer.*

Trajan interrogated him: 'Dost thou then bear the Crucified One in thy heart?'

'Even so,' came the answer, 'for it is written, "I will dwell in them, and walk in them, and I will be their God and they shall be my people."'

The Godbearer ... an honourable title for any Christian! We need more of us around, with lives that suggest we are carrying Jesus with us; finally destined to bear His likeness in heaven.

'What glory can the earth afford in comparison?'
(From a sermon by Charles Simeon of Cambridge, 1759-1836)

80

*'I will stand at my watch and station myself on the ramparts;
I will look to see what He will say to me'*
(Hab. 2:1)

Who are the strong ones when society is tottering? In May-June 605 BC a climactic battle had taken place by the river Euphrates, at Carchemish. There Nebuchadnezzar's army had smashed the Egyptians, and Babylon was the new world threat.

The prophet Habakkuk staggered under these convulsions, but found strength in staying at his post – and so inspired others. To *stand at your watch* implies vigilance; holding a newspaper in one hand, a Bible in the other – and getting on your knees.

We watch from a position of stability. Involvement in earth's struggles is inevitable, but prayer raised Habakkuk to 'the ramparts,' above the commotion, to a platform of strength.

We watch from a position of serenity. 'I will look to see what HE will say to me.' The prophet knew that human-based solutions will eventually collapse. It was with confidence that he was able to spread the confused situation before the *Lord*.

We watch from a position of authority. Believers are *not* helpless when great forces are unleashed upon the earth. We have a vantage point of unseen influence in the life with God!

'Christianity has never been scared of a revolution'
(Revival leader and Bishop, Festo Kivengere of Uganda)

81

'I am the bread of life'
(John 6:35)

Jesus has fed five thousand people from a boy's picnic. Now He uses the occasion to talk about true bread. Under Moses the people of Israel had lived on 'manna' in the wilderness. But this is different. The bread of old could only satisfy a nation; Jesus has come to satisfy *the world*. The bread of old could only satisfy the body; Jesus has come to satisfy *the soul*. The bread of old could only satisfy for a period; Jesus will satisfy *for ever*.

'Sir,' said Christ's listeners, 'From now on give us this bread!' They hadn't quite taken it in. Have you? *The bread that satisfies our inmost being is a Person,* a Person who has given His 'flesh' in death, so that we might live for ever (v. 51).

Let something else occupy the centre – and we will never be satisfied. The famed scientist Charles Darwin wrote to a friend, J.D. Hooker, on June 17th 1868: *I am glad you were at 'The Messiah'. It is the one thing I should like to hear again. But I dare say I should find my soul too dried up to appreciate it as in olden days. For it is a horrid bore to feel as I constantly do; that I am a withered leaf for everything, except science.*

Better was Martin Luther's experience, as he read John 6:35-

'Upon these words I will go to sleep at night'
(Martin Luther of Germany,
founder of the Reformation, 1483–1546)

82

'I am the light of the world'
(John 8:12)

Jesus would have stood in the light of several great golden candelabra when He uttered this awesome claim at Jerusalem's Feast of Tabernacles (John 7:37). The lamps reminded the people of the pillars of light that led them in their wanderings.

Now here was Jesus' claim - unique, universal and ultimate! Jesus was not claiming to be one of many lights that have guided humanity, but *the* Light; not simply the light and guide of Judaism, but of the *world*; not simply one *more* light, but original unborrowed Light in the absolute sense. John stated it clearly at the start of his gospel – *The true light that gives light to every man was coming into the world* (John 1:9). That is, no one who turns to Jesus – irrespective of culture or background – will remain in spiritual darkness!

Once recognize Christ as the Light – and we are changed for ever. It can happen anywhere. A musician I knew came to this great realization in the middle of a ballroom dance floor; she is now a missionary in Africa. An army soldier could find nowhere to kneel undisturbed in his surrender to Christ - except in the barracks bathroom. A hundred and fifty years ago the Rev. William Haslam 'felt a wonderful light' during one of his own sermons – and was converted in his own pulpit!

'The Lord Jesus is a sun which never sets'
(Augustine of Hippo, AD 354–430)

83

'I am the door'
(John 10:7 KJV)

The ancient city of Troy, made famous by Homer's account of the Trojan War, had but one door. You could keep circling its walls – but there was only one way in. In our passage, Jesus is taking the image not so much of a city, but of a middle eastern sheep pen…. Yet the principle is the same - of only one way in.

The door… the very gateway to life and safety – but why can't it be a case of 'One God – many doors?' *Problem:* no other 'doorway' can compare with that provided in the person of Jesus. Have any other candidates for the position beaten humanity's enemy, *Death?* Can any other applicants deal with the problem of *guilt* – that keeps sinners excluded? Are there any other aspirants who are morally *flawless?* If not, they are going to be in desperate need of a safe entry *themselves!*

It can only be this one Person … and He is big enough to take in those from every strata of society. *Further: while Jesus is the only door to God, there are many doors to Jesus.* I was driving once, and I gave a lift to a man of another belief-system. We got on well. 'I'd like to think,' I said as we finally parted, 'that your present beliefs will one day act as a stepping stone for you – towards Christ himself.'

'And that Thou bidd'st me come to Thee,
O Lamb of God, I come, I come!'
(From the hymn, 'Just as I Am', by Charlotte Elliott)

84

'I am the good shepherd'
(John 10:11)

Here is a fourth *I Am* from John's Gospel. Perhaps the emphasis should be on the word *good*. Too often spiritual leaders in the past were described as 'the shepherds who are destroying and scattering the sheep of my pasture' (Jer. 23:1). Elsewhere we read, 'I am against the shepherds and will hold them accountable for my flock' (Ezek. 34:10).

In Jesus' day it was evidently the Pharisees who were the 'thieves and robbers.' They were at best no more than 'hired hands' who – at the first sign of trouble – were up and away.

The 'good' shepherd gives *protection*, *direction* and *satisfaction* to the flock. He knows each one of His flock by name – and they know Him well enough to recognize and trust His voice; never that of a 'stranger' – be it of the world, the flesh or the Devil.

We knew this as young children growing up on the lower slopes of Mount Kenya – from Frances Ridley Havergal's hymn, 'God will take care of you,' set to the beautiful tune *O Quanta Qualia*. Here is the 'night-time' verse:

> *God will take care of you; all through the night*
> *Jesus, the Shepherd, His little one keeps;*
> *Darkness to Him is the same as the light;*
> *He never slumbers, and He never sleeps.*

85

'I am the resurrection and the life'
(John 11:25)

Here in John's Gospel, Jesus *says* it, He *does* it – and He *IS* it! He's at the graveside of a much-loved friend – who has been in the tomb for four long days. Jesus is more than a godly miracle-maker. He's utterly different from a wonder-worker who might say, 'I can turn water into wine, I can stop storms, I can multiply bread; listen – I can even do resurrections!'

No, Jesus is more than someone who dispenses wonderful gifts. *He IS the gift itself.* He is the original source of all life. He is the one and only universal Resurrection and the Life. You don't come to Jesus for *gifts*. You come because He is *Jesus*.

At the tomb they're weeping – and Jesus weeps too. So He doesn't look down upon our sorrows in calm detachment; He has emotions too. A friend of mine described her sense of outrage as the coffin of her father was lowered into the ground. Something inside her was shouting *That's my DADDY!* What a difference it makes that Jesus, Lord of all life, shares our grief.

In our story, Lazarus, the dead friend, was raised. This was not *The* Resurrection. Lazarus would die again. *But the event was a sign of things to come.* Later, Christ's own historic, bodily resurrection was a universal event, affecting everything. His resurrection is the prototype for every one of His friends.

He says it ... He does it ... He IS it ...

86

'I am the way, the truth and the life'
(John 14:6)

The Greek thinker Plato was so massive that all future strides in western thought were later described as a series of 'footnotes to Plato.' Yet even Plato wrote, *The Father of the world is hard to discover, and when discovered cannot be communicated.*

Thus when it comes to finding God there have been as many ways devised as there are people. In Katmandhu there are more gods than people, and more temples than houses. In the face of such plurality, is there a single convincing system of thought that can point the way through, and unite humanity?

The contention of the Christian faith is that we are utterly reliant upon the revelation made directly from heaven in the Person of the God-Man, Jesus Christ. 'How can we know the way?' asked Thomas, one of His twelve disciples.

The answer from Jesus assured him not only that the way lay in Himself, but also that there was *no other way*, for – He added - 'No one comes to the Father except through me.'

That revelation has created the widest family of belief ever.

'Without the way, there is no going.
Without the truth there is no knowing.
Without the life there is no living'
(Thomas à Kempis, 1379–1471)

87

'I am the true vine'
(John 15:1)

If you ever visit Hampton Court, near London – former grand home of some of England's famous monarchs – you are bound to come across the 'Great Vine' – the oldest of its kind in the world. It is fascinating to observe how the spreading branches of this gigantic vine derive their life from a single central stem. The vital *union* between a vine and its branches was used by Jesus to teach the utter dependence of His followers on Himself. And 'fruitfulness' is the very life of God, outpouring itself in Godlike character and selfless service. *Stay joined to Christ* is the message – and there will be fruit. It will just happen!

William Nagenda of Uganda was one of the most effective Christian leaders Africa has ever had. It was in his early days of unbelief that he was first challenged. 'Jesus sent four Africans to my town', he explained. 'I looked into their faces which were so full of joy and peace. I said to myself, "I wish I had such a face." I asked them what made the difference. They said, *"We have not done one thing to become different!"'* The explanation, they said, lay in the power of Christ. 'I couldn't believe it,' said William. 'That, to me, was a new Gospel.'

Be a part of the True Vine - and the supernatural work of God will do the rest. Test yourself one day from Galatians 5:22, 23!

'Apart from Me you can do nothing'
(Jesus' words in John 15:5)

88

Jesus, knowing all that was going to happen to him,
went out and asked them, 'Who is it you want?'
'Jesus of Nazareth,' they replied. 'I am he,' Jesus said. (And Judas
the traitor was standing there with them.) When Jesus said,
'I am he,' they drew back and fell to the ground.
(John 18:4-6)

Generally, it is held that there are seven instances of Christ's *'I AM'* phrase in John's Gospel, but here is a fascinating eighth. For the New Testament Greek has Jesus replying simply to his enemies, 'ego eimi' – literally, *I am.*

Coming as it did - at the arrest that inaugurated the long-awaited 'hour' of Christ's ordeal - the statement had the effect of a thunderclap. 'I am' is the *divine Name*, first announced to Moses (Exod. 3:14). Uttered now, and in such a manner, it highlighted the chasm between the majesty of Jesus and the treachery of Judas and his armed companions. As Gordon Bridger writes, 'A look. A word. The divine name; and they shrink from his presence.' Only then does Jesus allow them to take Him.

It's good to be on the side of Jesus – even when the worst things imaginable are happening. He is in charge. Always.

'If we really met him,
we too would fall to the ground'
(Gordon Bridger, *The Man from Outside*, Inter-Varsity Press)

89

'In Joppa there was a disciple named Tabitha....
who was always doing good'
(Acts 9:36)

How did this woman ever get into the Bible? She sewed, she helped the poor – and was loved. That was about it. My Kenya missionary 'aunt', Lorna Bowden, was rather like Tabitha. Out in the African bush she could innovate, and be fun. She made butterless, sugarless, flourless, eggless cakes ... and she did the injections. Once she had to inject a missionary, 'Uncle Harvey.' It was a little awkward; the injection had to be in his backside.

'Oh, Harvey, this is a bit ... difficult,' said a rather pink Aunty Lorna. 'Whatever are we going to do?'

'I tell you what, Lorna,' came the reply. 'I'll stand one side of the door, you the other and you can do it through the keyhole!'

Aunty Lorna was far more interesting to us than the boring 'White Mischief' settlers of *Happy Valley* – who treated the country as their playground and put nothing into it. Lorna's house decades later is still called *Miss Bowden's house* by the locals. She lived for others; they never forgot her. Maybe she *could* have got into the Bible, like Tabitha. Though Tabitha, remember, was raised from the dead! That certainly helped ...

'God uses men who are weak and feeble
enough to lean on him'
(Mission pioneer James Hudson Taylor, 1832–1905)

90

'As long as it is day, we must do the work of him who sent me.
Night is coming, when no-one can work.'
(John 9:4)

Perhaps it was these words of Jesus that inspired a family friend of ours under pressure – Ken Ogden. Ken was working in a 'difficult' part of Africa. One day he was told by the political authorities that he was to be expelled from the country; that he had twenty-four hours to get out.

How would you have spent those last twenty-four hours? Running round to the bank, to see if you could get your money out? Feverishly scraping your belongings together?

Ken had other ideas. As a builder he had been establishing a new church, along with his African colleagues. Everything was complete – except for the seats. There were none. Ken called his fellow-builders together and told them, 'I'll design and build with you just *one* seat for the new church. Then that seat can be the model for you to finish the rest. Let's get going – we haven't long!'

Twenty-four hours later Ken was out of the country, leaving behind a model for his friends to work from…but also a model of how a servant of Christ behaves when the going is rough.

'Lord, give me eyes to see, and grace to seize,
every opportunity for Thee'
(The daily prayer of
chaplain-general Bishop Taylor Smith, 1860–1937)

91

'I will pour out my Spirit on all people. Your sons and daughters will prophesy, your young men will see visions, your old men will dream dreams'
(Acts 2:17)

Dr Joe Church, known to me as 'Uncle Joe,' was used by God at the start of the great East African Revival. Empty and exhausted, he sat under a thorn tree on Ndera Hill in Rwanda. There he prayed for a fresh touch of the Holy Spirit upon himself and upon the surrounding dormant churches. 'The site of the beautiful spreading acacia tree seemed like holy ground,' wrote Patricia St John in her book *Breath of Life* (Norfolk Press, 1971). Eventually a church was built around the tree.

'One can specialize in medical research, surgery or translation,' agonized Joe, 'but what is the priority in it all?... I cannot see an inch ahead.' Joe was joined in his search by his hospital dresser Yosiyah Kinuka, and by Simeoni Nsibambi – both of whom I was later to meet. They pored over the Scriptures … and the answer began to emerge. *A heart wide open to God – transformed by the light and love and sweetness of the character of Jesus – and the Cross at the centre.* 'God met with me,' explained Joe, 'He gave me no special "gift."' But it was the start of a Revival that touched hundreds, then thousands and finally millions, across East Africa.

Be under your own 'acacia tree' tonight! Then *you* can pray:

'O God, bring a Revival – and begin it in me'

92

'Let the little children come to Me, and do not hinder them,
for the kingdom of God belongs to such as these'
(Mark 10:14)

A little girl of four was tucked up in bed. 'Now Katie,' her mother would say, 'you are not here in this world for yourself. You have been sent for God – and for others.' Then she would add, 'The world is waiting for you!' Her words were believed.

Young Kate's mother was Catherine, wife of General William Booth, founder of the Salvation Army. Kate became one of the most powerful mission workers and speakers who ever came out of Britain. By her teens, she was helping in her father's meetings, and could cope with the rowdiest of crowds. 'When all else fails,' enthused William, 'put on Katie!'

In her twenties she took a group of Salvation Army 'Hallelujah Lassies' with her into the dives and brothels of Paris – where her courage earned the military nickname of *La Marechale*. Once her boldness landed her in prison. Well into her nineties Kate travelled and spoke everywhere. It was said, 'She makes Jesus more real than anyone we have ever heard.' She would sign her name, 'Yours ever, in blood and fire! The Marechale.'

'Mother says the world is waiting for me.' That was the start!

'Nothing in this world matters
but what you have done for Jesus'
(Kate Booth, The Marechale, 1858–1955)

93

'Seeing the crowds, he went up on the mountain,
and when he sat down, his disciples came to him.
And he opened his mouth and taught them....'
(Matt. 5:1,2 ESV)

Put yourself in the crowd! *The Sermon on the Mount* is the most revolutionary piece of public oratory ever delivered. Robert Powell, who played the part of Jesus in Zeffirelli's film *Jesus of Nazareth*, was riveted by it.

'The setting was superb,' he declared, 'and I got carried away. The beauty of the words and ideas, when spoken aloud, are overwhelming. Half way through I started crying .... You can read the words in the Bible, but when you come to say them aloud, it's something else. They are electric.'

The salt of the earth, hiding your light, turning the other cheek, casting your pearls before swine, building on sand – people use these phrases daily. Here, Jesus is not telling us how to be saved. He is giving disciples a pen-picture of the life expected *of the saved person* - lived on the inside of God's kingdom; a 'blessed,' a *joyous* life!

Wait now for tomorrow - the first of eight 'beatitudes'.

Lord Jesus, I come to you tonight as my Teacher. Let me not live
life on the edge, but at the centre.

94

'Blessed are the poor in spirit, for theirs
is the kingdom of heaven'
(Matt.5:3)

Here is the first of eight 'beatitudes.' These are descriptions not of eight people, but eight sides of *one person* – the ideal believer who is blessed, or as we might say, 'congratulated.'

The first quality is poverty of spirit. Here is the very opposite of 'the self-made man.' Jesus is describing those who come in dependence upon God for everything - knowing the emptiness of their own inner character. They will say with the hymn-writer, *Nothing in my hand I bring; simply to Thy Cross I cling.*

Such humble dependence was illustrated in the life of a British industrialist, Sir John Laing, who attained international acclaim in the building of airfields, motorways – and numerous churches. A church I led at Harold Wood benefited from his generosity. Although he was 'rich' in the popular sense, money had no hold on him whatever, and he drove a second-hand car. *John Laing's riches were within.* Most of his fortune he gave away. When in 1978 this humble Christian man died, in his ninety-ninth year, his personal net estate came out at … £371.

A happy man? Completely. He lived for the interests of God and His kingdom. In this way, according to Jesus, he possessed the kingdom …. And it made him happy – and 'blessed.'

'The door into the kingdom is low'
(Scottish theologian Samuel Rutherford, 1600–1661)

95

'Blessed are those who mourn, for they will be comforted'
(Matt. 5:4)

Years ago I was about to take a funeral. 'Tell me about your husband,' I said to the widow. Her reply sent shivers down my spine: 'To Nobby, life was one jolly good binge!'

No problems then for the departed man about life here; its casualties, injustices and sins. Had *he* ever needed 'comfort'? No, he had created his own. A consumer - never a contributor – the world had been his playground. Such a tragedy can happen to anyone. You can be in church, and know nothing of Christ's second beatitude that stands hedonistic values on their heads.

Jesus' revolutionary teaching is that those who are aware of the surrounding pains of a fallen world, who indeed grieve over their own failures and sins, are in a happy position. The Lord is not primarily speaking of the loss of a loved one at this point. The 'mourning' here is one of personal repentance. There is such a thing as *godly sorrow*, and its happy sequel is salvation! (2 Cor. 7:10). Therein lies the 'comfort' of a life that – whatever its failures – is on the way *up*!

'I am not what I ought to be, I am not what I hope to be, I am not what I wish to be – but by the grace of God I am not what I was!'
(John Newton, 1727–1807)

96

'Blessed are the meek, for they will inherit the earth'
(Matt. 5:5)

It was Martin Luther, the great German reformer, who, when tempted to go down the road of pushy assertiveness, would mentally go to the front door of his life and say to the Tempter, 'Martin Luther is dead; Jesus Christ lives here.'

And there lies the key to this third beatitude of our Lord's, for Jesus encourages us to 'Take my yoke upon you and learn of me; *for I am meek and lowly in heart*' (Matt. 11:29 KJV). If Christ lives in us, then we have something of the true spirit of the servant King within. And to be meek is to be in control.

But can we really live like this? We can. Take the only English king - Alfred - who was ever called *The Great*. He was known everywhere as The Protector of the Poor. After receiving the surrender of Guthrum, heathen king of the invading Danes, Alfred made friends with him, *and invited the Danes to have a share in the land.* Such 'meekness' won Guthrum to Christ, and he was baptized – with Alfred as his godfather. Alfred was England's first great Christian king, and he 'inherited the earth,' for when he died in AD 890, he left England peaceful, stable and undeniably Christian – for centuries to come.

'When, through the growth of the Kingdom, the ungodly are weeded out from the earth, the meek are left to inherit it'
(From the commentary on Matthew's Gospel, by Alfred Plummer, 1915)

97

'Blessed are those who hunger and thirst for righteousness,
for they will be filled'
(Matt. 5:6)

I was once interviewing John Stott, in a public gathering, and my last question was, 'What are you looking forward to more than anything else?'

He replied, 'I think I can truthfully say that I look forward to being more like the Lord Jesus Christ in my character. That, above everything else.'

Wherever our present circumstances find us tonight – at home, travelling, in hospital or in a rest home – *this is what we were born for: Christ-likeness!* What was it about Jesus that pulled the crowds to Him from every quarter? It was His intrinsic, magnetic *goodness*. 'Goodness' sounds dull – yet it's only the goodness of fiction that's boring, while fictional evil exerts a strange fascination upon us all. *But real life turns the tables.* When you meet a really good person, you never want them to leave! And evil, in real life, is boring and flat – and never delivers. Ultimately it produces only a monotonous desert.

To thirst after righteousness is to want to be like Jesus. The satisfying result is *more* of Jesus, the source of all goodness.

'What more can the soul want than to be filled with Thee,
O God, who didst make us for thyself?'
(*The Directory of the Devout Life*, F.B. Meyer, 1847–1929)

98

'Blessed are the merciful, for they will be shown mercy'
(Matt. 5:7)

'William Nagenda can read my thoughts; it's a bit scary!'
I said to an African friend years ago. I was referring to the
Ugandan evangelist who was a leader in the great Revival
that transformed churches across East Africa.

'True,' came the reply. 'William can tell if you're out of
step with the Lord – but don't be scared; he's so humble that
the first sin he brings to light will always be his own!'

This is something of the principle that lies behind the fifth
beatitude of the Sermon on the Mount. It's the people who
know the forgiving power of God in their own needy lives
who can be relied on to show the same accommodating spirit
to others. *Mercy will be theirs at the final judgment.* It is not
that God's mercy towards us is a reward for our own mercy
to others. It is simply that once divine forgiveness has taken
hold of our hearts, we are never the same people again.

Look back on the day. Is there someone on whom you
should practise mercy? It should be second nature to every
believer.

*'Bear with each other and forgive whatever grievances you may
have against one another'*
(Col. 3:13)

99

'Blessed are the pure in heart, for they will see God'
(Matt. 5:8)

Liz and I were on *safari* in Kenya's Maasai Mara, gazing at a family of elephants. Suddenly the smallest one tripped on a tuft of grass and fell down, squealing. In an instant the entire family formed a protective circle round the baby – Mum, Dad, uncles, aunts, Grandad – trunks raised threateningly against any potential trouble. We glanced nervously at our Kenyan guide. One look at his tranquil face was enough – *no problem!*

When it comes to the Lord God, are we able to see *His* face? Jesus says we can. Not with full and open visibility; that will have to wait until the next life – but with the eyes of our spirit.

Here is a blessing, a *beatitude* that millions are experiencing every day. It is the inner knowledge that there is *'no problem'* surfacing between my God and myself – in spite of my past and every present hang-up, fantasy or addiction that may still torment me. The secret is, according to an old adage, *to keep short accounts with Christ;* to bring the failures and sins of every day into the light of the Cross, and to know that they are forgiven. If we confess those *known* sins to Him, we are assured from 1 John 1:9 that we are purified from *all* unrighteousness!

With the eyes of our spirit we may then look into His face, know for sure that there is *no problem* ... and tumble into bed.

Prayer: *'Create in me a pure heart, O God'*
(Ps. 51:10)

100

'Blessed are the peacemakers, for they will be called sons of God'
(Matt. 5:9)

Some people can walk onto the shop floor, into the common room, a building site or the church hall – and bring unity and peace with them. There are others – in every walk of life – who can create division and hassle every time they turn up. Review the last twelve hours and ask yourself whether you have inspired your friends or exhausted them!

Jesus is 'the Prince of Peace' (Isa. 9:6). By His death He created 'one new man' out of Jew and Gentile, *'thus making peace'* (Eph. 2:15). It is a peace offered, not imposed – and when His mission is rejected, then indeed it can act as a sword, dividing societies and whole families (Matt. 10:34-36). Yet, at a London church I worked in, we had some seventy different nationalities – with diverse clothing and a multiplicity of dialects. But a holy unity descended upon us. Jesus was big enough to hold us all together.

When we are involved in Christ's peace-making mission, we will be called children of God – not by Jesus (for He called us that when we first trusted Him; John 1:12) – but by outsiders who witness the power of Christ working through His friends.

'Lord, if I must dispute, let it be with the children of the devil!
Let me be at peace with thy children!'
(From John Wesley's Journals, July 20 1761)

101

'Blessed are those who are persecuted because of righteousness,
for theirs is the kingdom of heaven'
(Matt 5:10)

So the Beatitudes end with the promise given at the start: 'For theirs is the kingdom of heaven.' Followers of Christ are not to invite opposition - but should not be surprised if it comes, for they tread in the footsteps of their once-crucified Leader.

But why does Jesus go on to say (v. 12) 'Rejoice and be glad', when persecution comes? The answer is that the oppression of a faithful disciple is a bonus certificate – of genuineness! Acts 5:41 tells us that after the apostles had been flogged they were 'rejoicing because they had been counted worthy of suffering disgrace for the Name.' If you are being given a rough time as a Christian, *you are following in the true apostolic succession.*

Every piece of opposition is an extra, practical confirmation that the inheritance of the kingdom of heaven is yours.

And what if we are *not* suffering open persecution for our beliefs? First, *be on guard* 'when all men speak well of you, for that is how their fathers treated the false prophets' (Luke 6:26). But then we can open a dossier on Christians martyrs elsewhere – and so *identify* with our sisters and brothers.

'The messengers of Jesus will be hated to the end of time'
(Dietrich Bonhoeffer,
martyred under the Hitler regime, April 1945)

102

'In the night I remember your name, O Lord'
(Ps. 119:55)

Despite the popularity of many modern spiritual songs, there are certain hymns that outlast all the rest. One such is *The Day Thou Gavest, Lord, Is Ended.* Written in 1870, it was Queen Victoria's favourite hymn – with its reminder that prayer all over the world never stops.

> *As o'er each continent and island*
> *the dawn leads on another day,*
> *The voice of prayer is never silent,*
> *Nor dies the strain of praise away.*

This touches the imagination. Think of it: ours is the only planet, in all our millions of galaxies, where the Maker of the universe can be spoken to by living members of His creation.

Let it be a delight for us. Just a single word – spoken in the Name of Christ – and we are carried to the Throne. Ruth, wife of the evangelist Billy Graham, said that she would sometimes wake in bed, and discover that her husband was not beside her. He had slipped momentarily out of bed – onto his knees in prayer. Whether in bed or out of it, the same privilege is ours. Anxieties tend to multiply at night – but they dissipate with our wakened remembrance of the powerful Name of the Lord.

> *'The name of the Lord is a strong tower'*
> (Prov. 18:10)

103

'Our Father'
(Matt. 6:9)

Here is the beginning of *The Lord's Prayer*, and it begins with the 'Father' concept that is unique to Christianity. We don't grasp it easily. The early Gnostic heretics maintained that God was far too great to be bothered about the pathetic affairs of ordinary people. But Jesus taught differently. 'Are not two sparrows sold for a penny? Yet not one of them will fall to the ground apart from the will of your Father. And even the very hairs of your head are all numbered' (Matt. 10:29).

For followers of Jesus to say that God is their Father is more than saying we are the *creatures* of God. Your pet bird is that! It's more than saying that we are the *objects of divine love*, for God's providence extends to believers and unbelievers alike; the sun shines on the just and the unjust. It's more than saying that as part of humanity we are *derived* from God; that could be said of Hitler or Stalin. To some, Jesus even had to say, 'You are of your father the devil.'

No. Christ's death opened the door to the presence of God as someone we can run to and confide in as our intimate Father. Nor is He without the motherly characteristics of tenderness and sympathetic comfort. Can you call God 'Father?' *Try it.*

'Closeness, affection and generosity are at the heart of the relationship'
(J.I. Packer, *Knowing God*, Hodder)

104

'Who art in heaven'

Here is a second phrase of the Lord's Prayer. The best thing I ever saw was the Victoria Falls in Zimbabwe. This gigantic sight measures a mile across. No camera can contain its image.

What, then, of the God of the whole universe? The renowned king Solomon built a magnificent temple for Him, but was forced to concede, 'The heavens, even the highest heaven cannot contain You. How much less this temple I have built!'

The words 'in heaven' refer not exactly to the headquarters of God (because to localize Him is to limit Him) – but rather to indicate that the power at His command is universal. But the phrase also demonstrates the vast gulf between God and ourselves. We were made in His image – with the capacity for worship and fellowship with Him – *but in no way are we to be identified with God Himself.* Futile de-personalizing attempts to recast God as 'the ground of our being' and 'the ultimate within ourselves' can safely be consigned to the trashcans of the twentieth century. We are speaking of a 'Father', whose heartbeat of love has sustained His people throughout time.

> *'Father of Heaven, Whose love profound*
> *A ransom for our souls hath found,*
> *Before Thy throne we sinners bend;*
> *To us Thy pardoning love extend'*

(The Rev. Edward Cooper, 1805)

105

'Hallowed be thy Name'

Liz and I were going out to dine with our friends, William and Elinor Fitch. When we got to the restaurant it was crowded out; no more could be admitted. The couple in front of us was turned away. But not us. *'We're with Mr Fitch,'* we said.

Even on our human level there is a certain power about the right name! Come to the spiritual realm – and the Name of *The God and Father of our Lord Jesus Christ* has a power to inspire life-long missionary service and even martyrdom.

How burdened the ancient prophets had been, with their holy jealousy for the God of Abraham, Isaac and Jacob! How eloquent the Psalmist had been in his determination that 'from the rising of the sun to the place where it sets, the name of the LORD is to be praised' (Ps. 113:3). And then came Jesus who is none other than God in human form.... And faithful followers of His have not been afraid to brave all for the Name.

Other teachers and traditions might contribute whispers of truth, and even provide stepping stones towards Christ – the one way to the eternal Father. But only Jesus can rightly lay claim to universal allegiance. We are not to stop praying until that hallowed Name is acknowledged on all five continents. Be bold to bear and defend it yourself – publicly!

'... that worthy Name by which ye are called'

(James 2:7 KJV)

106

'Thy kingdom come'

Why is it that certain traditional eastern cultures have produced no significant historians? History, in some regions of the world is a blank. This is to be expected, because – according to some belief-systems – the visible world is an illusion and life is an endless circular process. However this is not the case when it comes to the faith of the Bible. M.D. Kingham's great hymn puts it clearly:

> God is working His purpose out, as year succeeds to year;
> God is working His purpose out, and the time is drawing near,
> Nearer and nearer draws the time, the time that shall surely be,
> When the earth shall be filled with the glory of God,
> as the waters cover the sea.

Is this kingdom territorial? No. Political? No. Military? No, never. Yet God's kingdom has outlived every institution going.

God HAS always ruled *eternally* – as King over nature and history. Yet He also DOES rule *redemptively*, through the coming of Jesus for fallen humanity – establishing the flag of His kingdom in lives everywhere. He WILL also rule *finally*, at the climactic end of time, when Christ returns and the last Judgment takes place. It is that 'end-time' rule that we are to pray for ... *and work for*, as we make the King known to others.

'What joy it is to plant His flag in another life'
(Guy H. King, who passed to Glory
the night after his final sermon, 1956)

107

'Thy will be done on earth as it is in heaven'

In the days of old-styled Communism in Eastern Europe, a Hungarian Christian used to pass the hated Party headquarters in Budapest every day on his way to work, and he would curse it.

One day God seemed to be telling him, 'Stop cursing that building. I may have plans for it. *Bless it for me instead.*' From that day on the man complied, and his attitude changed.

Weeks turned to months, and months to years. Then, at the end of the 1980s, the political change came. Suddenly the Communists were out of their building and a new use had to be found for it. Today it is a church, with hundreds of members. And who was the first pastor of the new church? Why, the man whose cursing turned to praying.

The wonder of this phrase in the Lord's Prayer is that humans can be as effective *here on earth* as the angels are in heaven, in establishing God's will.

Thy will be done can be prayed even in the darkest moments of the night. The happenings of every day can be placed under our Father's care. We pray. God works. It is His chosen way.

'All I asked of Him was that He should give me what He might think best for me'
(Letter by Erasmus, Dutch Renaissance scholar, 1466–1536)

108

'Give us this day our daily bread'

At this point in the Lord's Prayer, the emphasis switches from God's interests – His name, His rule, His will – to our own.

It is a basic petition. The word used for 'daily' is very rare in Greek literature. It was even thought that the New Testament writers had coined the word – until archeologists found it on an ancient papyrus fragment ... as part of a woman's shopping list. The German reformer Martin Luther interpreted *bread* to include 'everything necessary for the preservation of this life.'

It is an unselfish petition. The words 'us' and 'our' are vital; this is a corporate concern, for life is meant to be lived in relationship to others. The challenge of food today is not so much one of availability as of distribution and mutual care.

It is a humble petition. The test of our prayer life is not when things are going badly, but when they are going well. The assumption behind the petition is that, rain or shine, all life and strength and every heartbeat are dependent upon the Father in heaven.

A DAY AT A TIME. More days, more strength – *and no more than what is needed.* This surely has relevance today, wherever affluent and bloated communities are to be found.

'How many things there are that I do not want!'
(The Greek philosopher Socrates, 469–399 BC)

109

'And forgive us our trespasses, as we forgive those who trespass against us'

Devotees of every recognized belief-system need to be asked the vital question, 'On what basis do you hope to get forgiven?'

It is no answer to reply, 'Oh, God just forgives' – for that should prompt the immediate challenge, 'What, just like that? You're implying that six million people can go through the gas chambers and God can say, *That's all right, you're forgiven – let's say no more about it.* If forgiveness for you is as cheap as that, then the moral foundation of your faith is in question.'

The death of Jesus Christ, prefigured in the sacrificial system of the Old Testament, was a universal event – stretching in time backwards as well as forwards in its effect (Rev. 13:8), and is the only basis on which forgiveness can ever be granted to a repentant individual. It is never cheap. It is on this basis that we can pray, 'Forgive us our sins.'

The balancing phrase – 'as we forgive those who sin against us' – in no way implies that we have to *earn* forgiveness by our forgiveness of others. Rather, our willingness to forgive others, including our enemies, is one of the tell-tale *evidences* that the forgiveness of God has indeed reached into our very souls.

'To forgive one's enemies is the first, the most elementary characteristic of a Christian'
(Archbishop Anthony Bloom, *Living Prayer*)

110

'And lead us not into temptation,
but deliver us from evil'

The popular preacher Edward Reynolds (1599-1676) once said, 'Satan hath three titles given in the Scriptures, setting forth his malignity against the Church of God; a *dragon*, to note his malice; a *serpent*, to note his subtlety; and a *lion*, to note his strength. *But none of these can stand before prayer.*'

In point of fact, the opposition we face is not single but threefold – described traditionally as the World (all that entices us from outside), the Flesh (our inner fallen nature) and the Devil. Unbalanced teaching sometimes lumps all three categories into one – and blames the devil for everything.

Evil, then, is many-sided in its power to corrode a character – *and character is the only thing we can take into the next life.* The prayer that we will not be led into temptation is to be understood by the balancing phrase – 'but deliver us from evil.' God is not the source of temptation, but we shall certainly be faced by it. The prayer is that we will not be overwhelmed, but will find the way out (1 Cor. 10:13).

The battle is not one of power so much as motivation. It is through prayer, the Bible, Christian fellowship and worship that we can gain such a vision of Christ that we *want* to win.

'The devil slumbereth not, nor is the flesh yet dead'
(Thomas à Kempis, *The Imitation of Christ*)

111

'For thine is the kingdom, the power and the glory'

This final part of the Lord's Prayer is like an extra *coda*, echoed in praise from early Christian liturgies through to the soaring cadences of singers such as Huw Priday of Wales.

But the soul can sing too. To go along simply with a scientific explanation of our existence is to become completely dwarfed. Here is a 'medium-sized planet' on the edge of a constellation that is itself only one of countless constellations. Further, we are told that humanity itself has only been around for an infinitesimally small proportion of the life-span of the universe.

But the Bible turns all that on its head. The aeons of time during which the crustaceans and mosses came into being and the mountains were formed? *Let's call it a week's work.* Give it a page in the Scripture record. Correction – give it two pages! The stars? Five words will do, 'He made the stars also.' But *the real story* – the emergence of a people made in God's image; the establishing of God's kingdom in the lives of men and women who will praise His Name worldwide – why, we'll need a thousand pages for that, before we're through!

That's the true, the divine perspective. Sleep on it tonight, and rise in the morning with a song of the kingdom in your soul.

'The kingdom that we seek is the kingdom of heaven, not of men. Anything we touch we spoil'
(Dr Michael Green, *New Life, New Lifestyle*)

112

'For ever and ever, Amen'

Is That It? was the title of a book by Sir Bob Geldof. The title was based on a question put to Geldof by some onlookers at the close of a memorable charity concert that he had hosted at London's Wembley Stadium. Now that it was over, what then? *'Is that it?'* The final sentence of Geldof's book read, 'I've been asking myself the same question ever since.'

There has always been a wistful 'Now what?' element about a great deal of human-based achievement. The contention of Christianity is that eternal significance and direction is imparted to everything done for God. To be able to view our *ultimate* goal clearly puts satisfying meaning into the *present*.

Thus the final phrase of the Lord's Prayer reminds us that life with God is the *one thing* that is permanent. And to know Christ – the author of the prayer that we have been meditating upon – is to have established the link with Eternity itself.

'Ithe witu iguru ...'. How often as the child of missionaries I heard the opening words of the Lord's Prayer in the Kikuyu language! The timeless words, given us by the Man of Galilee, have been uttered across many centuries – in great cathedrals, tinned-roof churches and football stadiums; above countless graves and by hospital bedsides. Will you use them tonight?

> *'... Take prayer into every day – as a way of life'*
> (Sir Cliff Richard)

113

*'But thou, O man of God, flee these things; and follow after
righteousness, godliness, faith, love, patience, meekness.
Fight the good fight of faith'*
(1 Tim. 6:11,12 KJV)

'Flee ... Follow ... Fight!' Much of successful Christian living
requires us to *do* something. Negatively, to *Flee*; positively, to
Follow; actively, to *Fight*. When we give up on daily decisions
of this nature as being too inconvenient, then spiritually we are
into static middle-age. Some become middle-aged at twenty-
five, while others are still youthful at seventy and eighty.

What to *do* when tempted? A little girl replied, 'Oh, I send
Jesus to the door!' Good – for a ten-year-old. But the truth is
that Jesus sends *us* to the door – armed and motivated: 'Sorry,
Devil, not today.' It is as simple, and as inconvenient as that.

An example. The stakes have been raised in recent years over
the homosexual lifestyle. Throughout the debate, those whose
interests have been almost completely ignored are the bravest
and most honourable of all: they are men and women who
experience same-sex attractions, but continue in the life of the
church to fight – successfully – for the very purity of Jesus.

Whether it's ethics on the *macro* level of business, politics
or money transactions - or on the *micro* level of personal
lifestyle, there will be no let-up in the good fight of faith, to
the very end.

Stay on in the fight – and stay young!

114

'Be sober; be vigilant; because your adversary the devil, as
a roaring lion, walketh about, seeking whom he may devour:
Whom resist steadfast in the faith'
(1 Pet. 5:8 KJV)

As a student, my mother was the first-ever treasurer of what
was then called the Inter-Varsity Fellowship. Now it has gone
world-wide, but in those early, heady days, my mum kept the
entire proceeds of the IVF in a biscuit tin under her bed. She
took part in Bible meetings and missions. She was a dedicated
Christian worker, and eventually became a missionary.

Years ago she told me, 'The time to be spiritually alert is
when the pressures are off, after a demanding event that has
taken all your prayer and energy. "Mission accomplished" –
you're relaxed and happy. It's just *then* – with your guard down
– that you can be wide open to the seductive power of evil.'

Noah provides an example. With the adventure of the
Flood safely over, we soon find him blind drunk! Take
King David. At the height of his power, having crushed the
Arameans, he falls into immorality – and then, murder. Look
at the prophet *Elijah*; having routed 850 false prophets, his
morale collapses at the threat of one woman, Jezebel – and
he takes flight.

How are *you* doing right now? Pretty well? *Then stay on
guard.*

'Nothing fails like Success'
(Dean Inge of St Paul's Cathedral, London, 1860–1954)

115

'Be alert and keep on praying for all the saints'
(Eph. 6:18)

Who is praying for you? Do you know? And who are you praying for? *Here is mutual protection.* 'I pray for you on the nineteenth day of each month!' So said an Australian bishop to me years ago. I was astounded. This busy man, with all his responsibilities, was praying for *me!*

Question: How did the apostle Paul ever remember the *names* of all those people he greeted in his letters? It can only have been because he was praying for them constantly.

Have you got some kind of a prayer diary going? With names, Christian organisations and churches for which you have a concern? Perhaps you know of just *one* Christian leader in, say, Tanzania, who can come onto your prayer list – maybe on the nineteenth day of the month! Naturally we can pray spontaneously 'out of the heart' – but a small notebook, with enough pages to last a month, will *expand* our prayer life!

Ever been in a 'prayer triplet' of trusted friends, with whom you can get together periodically for prayer, perhaps at breakfast? Many people do it. In that way we can keep 'alert' and afford each other *the protection* that only prayer can give.

'As for me, God forbid that I should sin against the LORD in
ceasing to pray for you'
(1 Sam. 12:23 KJV)

116

'Wherewithal shall a young man cleanse his way?
by taking heed thereto according to thy word …
Thy word have I hid in mine heart,
that I might not sin against thee'
(Ps. 119:9,11 KJV)

Redd Harper, cowboy star of the film *Mr Texas*, cheerfully spoke of how he resisted evil: *'Get thee behind me Satan, while I look it up.'* We smile – but the principle is a tested one. If we know the Scriptures we have a bottomless resource at hand.

Without the Bible we cannot gain a conception of Jesus that will keep us 'cleansed' – or indeed enable us to withstand opposing world-views. There are those of other belief-systems who know the Bible better than many Christians – simply in order to out-argue the ill-equipped. Happy times in a youth concert will avail us nothing when faced by a determined and informed opponent of the faith. *Our* job is to win *them*!

We are not only to out-think our contemporaries, but also to *out-live* them. I once asked a man of another religion what had brought him to a Christian outreach event. He pointed at a slightly-built young man nearby. 'I'm here because of *him*.' He had been profoundly impressed by his 'pure' life-style.

The Bible, read daily – *and carried on our persons into the day* – is an open secret of success. Please join the club!

Let us be known everywhere as people of The Book.

117

'Peter followed Him at a distance'
(Mark 14:54)

Fellowship is vital if disciples of Jesus are to stay firm and clear-sighted. We could title this episode in the life of Peter as the anatomy of a spiritual collapse. When the crisis moment came at Jesus' arrest, we find Peter the Rock Man:

Disorientated. 'Simon, are you asleep?' (Mark 14:37) It was a bewildering moment for the drowsy apostle, as the guards closed in. Blindly striking out, he was a fumbling giant.

Distanced. Peter had become separated from John, when they reached the High Priest's house. Now he's sitting with the wrong people. *The isolated believer is the vulnerable believer.*

Disguised. There is a case for going into alien territory, but not if you are going to keep your spiritual allegiance concealed.

Dissociated. Suddenly the mask is torn from Peter's face. He dodges the question of his allegiance with a lie and a denial.

Discredited. Now he's stumbling out into the early hours of Friday, crucifixion day ... and weepingly he's out of it all. Yes, he got back eventually – *but none of this need have happened.*

*'I do not think the New Testament contemplates the
existence of unattached Christians'*
(*Studies in Theology*, Professor James Denney of Scotland,
1856–1917)

118

*'Offer your bodies as living sacrifices, holy and pleasing to God
– this is your spiritual act of worship'*
(Rom. 12:1)

People give their 'hearts' to the Lord, but – *bodies* – here is
very earthy language. Where are your eyes looking? What is
your mouth saying? What are your ears listening to? Where
are your feet taking you? As a boy I would be challenged by
talks at *'camp'*: 'Is Christ Lord of your diary ... of your money
box ... of your bedroom?' Get all this right, says Paul, and you
will be 'pleasing' God in this, your day's *worship*.

This is a daily delight for every believer: to present
ourselves – our little frame! – for use and service on the only
inhabited planet in all God's universe. And if you can *sing*
– without rousing or embarrassing others near you – why
not? A colleague I have worked with, John Cook, told me of
a Rwandan bishop and his wife who stayed with him during
a time of exile – and he would hear them singing hymns softly
together in their bedroom at the crack of dawn. *Worship!*

There's also worship with others: in the home group, the
sports fellowship, in the wider church ... always with the
reminder that you are not alone. This is going to hold you
– and keep your vision of Jesus fresh and *bright!*

'God doesn't want your cleverness; He wants your cleanness'
(Dr Alan Redpath, *Captivity to Conquest*)

119

'By His wounds we are healed'
(Isa. 53:5)

People down the centuries – including myself – have found forgiveness of their sins and peace with God through Isaiah 53 - the foretelling of God's coming 'righteous servant,' who 'was wounded for our transgressions.' Yes, the prophecy is of Jesus.

But in the light of verse 5 some wonder, *In addition to forgiveness of sins, is physical healing also a benefit of the death of Christ? Can I receive healing, as I can receive forgiveness?*

Although direct healing from God can and does happen at times, the answer in this instance seems to be *No.*

A wonderful evening of healings is recorded in Matthew 8, and reference is indeed made to Isaiah 53:5 – but this happened at Capernaum, long before the Cross had taken place. It would seem to be a reference to the overall coming of Jesus in the *Incarnation* – God in human form, sympathizing and identifying with the burdens of humanity. But later, when the apostle Peter quotes from Isaiah 53:5, he applies it directly to Christ's bearing of '*our sins* in his body on the tree' (1 Pet. 2:24). *Yet physical healings have occurred* – right up to today. What is their pattern? Let's save this topic for tomorrow...

'Physical health in a damaged universe is a mercy, not a right'
(David MacInnes, 'Today' magazine, April 1984)

120

'Now there is in Jerusalem near the sheep gate a pool,
which in Aramaic is called Bethesda'
(John 5:2)

Bible critics doubted the pool's existence – until 1876, when the excavators dug it up. It is visible today, with all five of the 'colonnades' mentioned in verse 2. Many invalids would gather at the pool, which was supposed to have had healing properties. Then one day Jesus came by – and a man disabled for thirty-eight years was healed – by a word from the Lord.

Jesus' healings were simple – He needed no roadshow, no stage, music or special lighting. These were acts of love, but they were also *selective*. No one else by the pool was healed that day. The reason is that it wasn't primarily for the temporary healing of the sick that Jesus came. All would die one day anyway – and then what of the next generation? No; John sees in these events authenticating 'signs' of Christ's divine identity.

At every stage of God's revelation this pattern is evident. Miracles feature strongly at the giving of *the Law* in Moses' time; at the beginning of *the Prophets*, with Elijah; at the time of *the Gospel* with Jesus; and at the coming of the *Spirit*, with the apostles. With each new development God seems to say, *Here are signposts to My true messengers*. But what about healing at other times? And today? Let's take that tomorrow.

'Not all are healed; else how should we ever die?'
(Guy H. King)

121

*'It is by the name of Jesus Christ of Nazareth,
whom you crucified but who God raised up from the dead,
that this man stands before you healed'*
(Acts 4:10)

Here is an example of a dramatic healing being used by God to authenticate His messengers at a new stage of Christian revelation. It gave the apostles Peter and John an opportunity to proclaim Christ – and Acts 4:18 reveals that what really upset the authorities was not the miracle but the preaching!

Do such healings happen today? They do – but we should not be surprised that they happen mostly on the boundary outposts of Christian mission, where there is little Bible heritage and where the messengers of the Gospel have yet to be recognized.

They may not occur so much in areas of prolonged Christian influence, or indeed of advanced medical science.

For while miracles can happen anywhere, we recognize that in the early development of medicine and of hospitals (largely begun by Christians), we are but fulfilling the original *divine* command to govern the world and husband its resources. Thus, if you are reading this as a hospital patient, thank God tonight for his healing powers at work in you! A heart by-pass? An appendectomy? These are modern miracles of God!

*'He deals with each person according to His infinite knowledge
of what is right and best'*
(Henry Frost, *Miraculous Healing*,
Christian Focus Publications)

122

'Is any one of you sick? He should call the elders of the church to pray over him and anoint him with oil in the name of the Lord... the Lord will raise him up'
(James 5:14,15)

'When did you start to lose your peace and have these bad dreams and hallucinations?' I asked one of our church members years ago. We tracked it down to a questionable public healing event, at which she had gone forward. Peace flooded back only after our friend renounced her action, and as we prayerfully placed the issue in Christ's hands.

When it comes to prayer for healing, the best platform of all is in *the local church*. It is there that we are known, where there is proper accountability and where there is ample opportunity for ongoing assessment and follow-up.

Prayer can happen within the local home group, at the hospital bedside or indeed on the basis of James 5:14-16 – when trusted leaders come to pray with the ill person – with the initiative coming from the *patient*. The 'elders' pray *over him*; so this is more than a trivial case. The 'oil' – symbolic of the Holy Spirit – also implies that medicine and prayer go together. Many times I have said after prayer of this kind, 'The Lord will raise you up; *it says so.*' In what specific *way* this may happen we must leave with the Lord himself. *But it is in His safe hands.*

> *'The essence of prayer is "Thy will be done"'*
> (J. Alec Motyer, *The Tests of Faith*, IVP)

123

'Behold, I stand at the door, and knock:
if any man hear my voice, and open the door,
I will come in to him, and will sup with him, and he with me.'
(Rev. 3:20 KJV)

Having been brought up in Kenya, there is a word spoken across East Africa, that I have always known, spoken from the open doorway of our various homes. Many times! One word:

Hodi

You say *Hodi* ('Hoddee') when you are seeking entry to a friend's house. It is never uttered in a loud, demanding voice, but in a tone of shy respect and gentle trust. You are saying, in effect, *'I'm here....Would you wish me to enter?'* The reply is 'Karibu!' In the Kikuyu language I grew up with, it is 'Uka!'

It is with that tone of friendly approach that Jesus Christ, very God of very God, once crucified for our sins and now raised as Lord of the universe, stands at the door of every life. He will never storm the citadel of our souls. He is waiting, hand on the knocker. *Hodi,* He says. What shall *we* say this evening?

A Prayer: Lord Jesus Christ, Thank you for waiting so long for me. I now take this moment to make firm my decision to receive you as my Saviour and Lord. I trust your promise that you have come into my life. Amen.

Christian Focus Publications

Our mission statement –

STAYING FAITHFUL
In dependence upon God we seek to impact the world through
literature faithful to His infallible Word, the Bible. Our aim
is to ensure that the Lord Jesus Christ is presented as the only
hope to obtain forgiveness of sin, live a useful life and look
forward to heaven with Him.

Our Books are published in four imprints:

CHRISTIAN
FOCUS

popular works including
biographies, commentaries, basic
doctrine and Christian living.

CHRISTIAN
HERITAGE

books representing some of
the best material from the rich
heritage of the church.

MENTOR

books written at a level suitable
for Bible College and seminary
students, pastors, and other
serious readers. The imprint
includes commentaries,
doctrinal studies, examination
of current issues and church
history.

CF4•K

children's books for quality Bible
teaching and for all age groups:
Sunday school curriculum, puzzle
and activity books; personal
and family devotional titles,
biographies and inspirational
stories – Because you are never
too young to know Jesus!

Christian Focus Publications Ltd,
Geanies House, Fearn, Ross-shire,
IV20 1TW, Scotland, United Kingdom.
www.christianfocus.com